Interpersonal Psychotherapy

Theories of Psychotherapy Series

Theories of Psychotherapy Series
Jon Carlson and Matt Englar-Carlson, Series Editors

Interpersonal Psychotherapy

Ellen Frank and Jessica C. Levenson

American Psychological Association

Washington, DC

First Printing July 2010
Second Printing July 2016
Third Printing January 2019

Published by
American Psychological Association
750 First Street, NE
Washington, DC 20002
www.apa.org

To order
APA Order Department
P.O. Box 92984
Washington, DC 20090-2984
Tel: (800) 374-2721;
Direct: (202) 336-5510
Fax: (202) 336-5502;
TDD/TTY: (202) 336-6123
Online: www.apa.org/books/
E-mail: order@apa.org

In the U.K., Europe, Africa, and the
Middle East, copies may be ordered from
American Psychological Association
3 Henrietta Street
Covent Garden, London
WC2E 8LU England

Typeset in Minion by Shepherd, Inc., Dubuque, IA

Printer: United Book Press, Baltimore, MD
Cover Designer: Minker Design, Sarasota, FL
Cover Art: *Lily Rising*, 2005, oil and mixed media on panel in craquelure frame, by Betsy Bauer

The opinions and statements published are the responsibility of the authors, and such opinions and statements do not necessarily represent the policies of the American Psychological Association.

Library of Congress Cataloging-in-Publication Data

Frank, Ellen, 1944–
  Interpersonal psychotherapy/Ellen Frank and Jessica C. Levenson.—1st ed.
    p. ; cm. — (Theories of psychotherapy series)
  Includes bibliographical references and index.
  ISBN-13: 978-1-4338-0851-7 (alk.paper)
  ISBN-10: 1-4338-0851-X (alk. paper)
  ISBN-13: 978-1-4338-0852-4 (e-book: alk. paper)
  ISBN-10: 1-4338-0852-8 (e-book: alk. paper) 1. Interpersonal psychotherapy.
I. Levenson, Jessica C. II. American Psychological Association. III. Title. IV. Series:
Theories of psychotherapy series.
  [DNLM: 1. Psychotherapy—methods. 2. Interpersonal Relations. 3. Mental
Disorders—therapy. WM 420 F8275i 2011]
  RC489.I55F73 2011
  616.89'14—dc22
                          2010019767

British Library Cataloguing-in-Publication Data
A CIP record is available from the British Library.

Printed in the United States of America
First Edition

Contents

Series Preface

Some might argue that in the contemporary clinical practice of psychotherapy, evidence-based intervention and effective outcome have overshadowed theory in importance. Maybe. But, as the editors of this series, we don't propose to take up that controversy here. We do know that psychotherapists adopt and practice according to one theory or another because their experience, and decades of good evidence, suggests that having a sound theory of psychotherapy leads to greater therapeutic success. Still, the role of theory in the helping process can be hard to explain. This narrative about solving problems helps convey theory's importance:

> Aesop tells the fable of the sun and wind having a contest to decide who was the most powerful. From above the earth, they spotted a man walking down the street, and the wind said that he bet he could get his coat off. The sun agreed to the contest. The wind blew and the man held on tightly to his coat. The more the wind blew, the tighter he held. The sun said it was his turn. He put all of his energy into creating warm sunshine and soon the man took off his coat.

What does a competition between the sun and the wind to remove a man's coat have to do with theories of psychotherapy? We think this deceptively simple story highlights the importance of theory as the precursor to any effective intervention—and hence to a favorable outcome. Without a guiding theory, we might treat the symptom without understanding the role of the individual. Or we might create power conflicts with our clients and not understand that, at times, indirect means of helping (sunshine) are often as effective—if not more so—than direct ones (wind). In the absence of theory, we might lose track of the treatment rationale and instead get caught up in, for example, social correctness and not wanting to do something that looks too simple.

What exactly *is* theory? The *APA Dictionary of Psychology* defines theory as "a principle or body of interrelated principles that purports to explain or predict a number of interrelated phenomena." In psychotherapy, a theory is a set of principles used to explain human thought and behavior, including what causes people to change. In practice, a theory creates the goals of therapy and specifies how to pursue them. Haley (1997) noted that a theory of psychotherapy ought to be simple enough for the average therapist to understand but comprehensive enough to account for a wide range of eventualities. Furthermore, a theory guides action toward successful outcomes while generating hope in both the therapist and client that recovery is possible.

Theory is the compass that allows psychotherapists to navigate the vast territory of clinical practice. In the same ways that navigational tools have been modified to adapt to advances in thinking and ever-expanding territories to explore, theories of psychotherapy have changed over time. The different schools of theories are commonly referred to as waves, the first wave being psychodynamic theories (i.e., Adlerian, psychoanalytic), the second wave learning theories (i.e., behavioral, cognitive–behavioral), the third wave humanistic theories (person-centered, gestalt, existential), the fourth wave feminist and multicultural theories, and the fifth wave postmodern and constructivist theories. In many ways, these waves represent how psychotherapy has adapted and responded to changes in psychology, society, and epistemology as well as to changes in the nature of psychotherapy itself. Psychotherapy and the theories that guide it are dynamic and responsive. The wide variety of theories is also testament to the different ways in which the same human behavior can be conceptualized (Frew & Spiegler, 2008).

It is with these two concepts in mind—the central importance of theory and the natural evolution of theoretical thinking—that we developed the Theories of Psychotherapy Series. Both of us are thoroughly fascinated by theory and the range of complex ideas that drive each model. As university faculty members who teach courses on the theories of psychotherapy, we wanted to create learning materials that not only highlight the essence of the major theories for professionals and professionals in training but also clearly bring the reader up to date on the current status of the models. Often in books on theory, the biography of the original theorist overshadows the evolution of the model. In contrast, our intent is to highlight the contemporary uses of the theories as well as their history and context.

As this project began, we faced two immediate decisions: which theories to address and who best to present them. We looked at graduate-level theories of psychotherapy courses to see which theories are being taught, and we explored popular scholarly books, articles, and conferences to determine which theories draw the most interest. We then developed a dream list of authors from among the best minds in contemporary theoretical practice. Each author is one of the leading proponents of that approach as well as a knowledgeable practitioner. We asked each author to review the core constructs of the theory, bring the theory into the modern sphere of clinical practice by looking at it through a context of evidence-based practice, and clearly illustrate how the theory looks in action.

There are 24 titles planned for the series. Each title can stand alone or can be put together with a few other titles to create materials for a course in psychotherapy theories. This option allows instructors to create a course featuring the approaches they believe are the most salient today. To support this end, APA Books has also developed a DVD for each of the approaches that demonstrates the theory in practice with a real client. Many of the DVDs show therapy over six sessions. Contact APA Books for a complete list of available DVD programs (http://www.apa.org/pubs/videos).

In *Interpersonal Psychotherapy*, Ellen Frank and Jessica Levenson provide a thorough review of how interpersonal psychotherapy (IPT) is ideally suited for the contemporary clinical climate that focuses on evidence-based practice. The authors outline the ironic origins of IPT, noting how this model was initially developed as a theoretical placebo for psychotherapy research. The promising outcomes from this placebo led to the creation of IPT as a stand-alone treatment for depression and other clinical concerns. As a time-limited approach, IPT is unique in that the clinical focus is less on the internal or intrapsychic and more on the interpersonal and social world of the client. The authors guide the reader through the theoretical foundations of the approach and the clinical stages of treatment by the use of detailed case examples and clinical illustrations. IPT is a widely researched approach, and the authors also examine the existing empirical data supporting its use across different populations and presenting concerns. The extensive empirical support for IPT makes this volume of the Theories of Psychotherapy Series particularly useful for students and clinicians.

—Jon Carlson and Matt Englar-Carlson

REFERENCES

Frew, J., & Spiegler, M. (2008). *Contemporary psychotherapies for a diverse world.* Boston, MA: Lahaska Press.

Haley, J. (1997). *Leaving home: The therapy of disturbed young people.* New York, NY: Routledge.

How to Use This Book With APA Psychotherapy Videos

Each book in the Theories of Psychotherapy Series is specifically paired with a DVD that demonstrates the theory applied in actual therapy with a real client. Many DVDs feature the author of the book as the guest therapist, allowing students to see an eminent scholar and practitioner putting the theory he or she writes about into action.

The DVDs have a number of features that make them excellent tools for learning more about theoretical concepts:

- Many DVDs contain six full sessions of psychotherapy over time, giving viewers a chance to see how clients respond to the application of the theory over the course of several sessions.
- Each DVD has a brief introductory discussion recapping the basic features of the theory behind the approach demonstrated. This allows viewers to review the key aspects of the approach about which they have just read.
- DVDs feature actual clients in unedited psychotherapy sessions. This provides a unique opportunity to get a sense of the look and feel of real psychotherapy, something that written case examples and transcripts cannot always convey.
- There is a therapist commentary track that viewers may choose to play during the psychotherapy sessions. This track gives unique insight into why therapists do what they do in a session. Further, it provides an in vivo opportunity to see how the therapist uses the model to conceptualize the client.

The books and DVDs together make a powerful teaching tool for showing how theoretical principles affect practice. In the case of *Interpersonal Psychotherapy*, the DVD *Interpersonal Psychotherapy for Older Adults With Depression*, featuring Gregory A. Hinrichsen, provides a vivid example of how this approach looks in practice.

Acknowledgments

Portions of this work were adapted from the following publications:

Klerman, G. L., Weissman, M. M., Rounsaville, B. J., & Chevron, E. S. (1984). *Interpersonal psychotherapy of depression:* New York, NY: Basic Books.

Weissman, M. M. (2006). A brief history of interpersonal psychotherapy. *Psychiatric Annals, 36,* 553–557.

Weissman, M. M., Markowitz, J. C., & Klerman, G. L. (2000). *Comprehensive guide to interpersonal psychotherapy.* New York, NY: Basic Books.

Weissman, M. M., Markowitz, J. C., & Klerman, G. L. (2007). *Clinician's quick guide to interpersonal psychotherapy.* New York, NY: Oxford University Press.

The authors would like to thank Elizabeth Didie, Laura Dietz, Tina Goldstein, Stephanie Hlastala, Jennifer Johnson, Ellen Poleshuck, Nancy Talbot, and Marian Tanofsky-Kraff for the information they each provided about their adaptations of interpersonal psychotherapy (IPT) for special populations. Thank you also to Debra Frankel for her assistance with the longer case example and to Marc Blom, John Markowitz, Hiroko Mizushima, Paula Ravitz, and Myrna Weissman for the information they provided on the history of the development and dissemination on IPT.

Interpersonal
Psychotherapy

1

Introduction

T he primary goal of this volume is to introduce readers to the theory and practice of interpersonal psychotherapy (IPT), with the hope that it may be adopted as their own and integrated into their repertoire of therapeutic tools. We hope that over time, the use of IPT in clinical settings will increase, so that the gains made by clients receiving IPT in research protocols and in the relatively circumscribed number of clinical settings where it is used routinely will generalize to those in a much wider range of therapeutic venues.

In our laboratory and in many others conducting research on IPT, the clinicians who provide the treatment include clinical psychologists, social workers, nurse clinicians, and psychiatry residents. Based on the success of each of these practitioners in implementing IPT, we are confident that clinicians with diverse backgrounds working in a variety of therapeutic settings will not only find it easy to integrate the principles of IPT into their work, but that they, too, will have success using this modality.

A BRIEF DESCRIPTION OF IPT

Interpersonal psychotherapy (Klerman, Weissman, Rounsaville, & Chevron, 1984; Weissman, Markowitz, & Klerman, 2000, 2007) is a focused treatment for depression and other disorders that focuses on the intersection of interpersonal dysfunction and psychiatric symptoms. The theoretical rationale of IPT rests on the idea that psychiatric disorders occur in an interpersonal context. All parts of the treatment repeatedly aim to connect the development of the individual's symptoms to his or her social circumstances. Through IPT, the client learns how to resolve the existing interpersonal challenge(s), how to anticipate future interpersonal concerns, and how resolution of these problems will contribute to the amelioration of his or her current symptoms and the prevention of future symptoms.

IPT is typically offered as a short-term treatment, although the long-term use of IPT has been found to be appropriate and efficacious in some clinical contexts. In its original conceptualization, short-term IPT generally lasts 16 to 20 sessions (Klerman et al., 1984; Weissman et al., 2000, 2007). While this format may limit the exploration of some areas in much depth, the time-limited nature of treatment motivates both client and therapist to stay on task and encourages the client to make changes. IPT may be used successfully when treating individuals of a variety of ages, cultural backgrounds, and psychiatric diagnoses. The client's previous relationships inform the therapist's understanding of the client's current situation; however, treatment typically focuses on present concerns in a collaborative atmosphere that integrates both the therapist's and client's goals and conceptualizations. In addition to the connection between interpersonal relationships and psychopathology, other unique aspects of IPT are the active stance of the therapist, who guides sessions with warm support of the client, the conceptualization of the client's psychopathology within a medical model, and the assigning of the client's difficulties to one of four interpersonal problem areas: unresolved grief, role transitions, role disputes, and interpersonal deficits (Klerman et al., 1984; Weissman et al., 2000, 2007). These unique IPT concepts will be explained in more detail in later chapters.

The theoretical basis of IPT is derived from the work of individuals in the interpersonal schools of psychology and psychiatry, such as Adolf Meyer, Harry Stack Sullivan, John Bowlby, Freida Fromm-Reichmann, and Mabel Blake Cohen (Klerman et al., 1984; Weissman et al., 2000). These individuals discussed how problems in interpersonal relationships may be related to psychopathology, either through experiences that originate during early development or through challenges faced in adulthood. These theorists explored how psychopathology may be related to social attachments, social support, and interpersonal life events. The client is seen as a social being, one who is affected by interpersonal experiences. Thus, it is logical that IPT asserts that a client's social circumstances have a large impact on his or her psychological state.

THE USE OF IPT FOR TREATING DEPRESSION

Based on this foundation, IPT is well suited to the treatment of depression. If we view depressive symptoms as arising in relation to difficulties in interpersonal relationships, social roles, social support, or social attachments, as proposed by the theorists of the interpersonal schools, these issues appear to be appropriate treatment targets for depressive symptoms.

IPT was originally developed as a treatment for depression within the context of a research project early in the psychopharmacologic drugs era. An early form of IPT was originally included in this research study of pharmacology, simply because of the presence of psychotherapy in clinical practice at the time. This early form of IPT was thought to have only a "milieu effect" on the patient's outcome, as the experimenters were not convinced that they would find a psychotherapy effect (Weissman, 2006). Yet, when the psychotherapy proved to be a success, the researchers developed this early form of IPT into a formal treatment. This original research study will be described in more detail in Chapter 2.

Some of the other characteristics that make IPT appropriate for treating depression include the identification, naming, and normalization of the disorder. Many individuals with depression find relief when they have a name for their disparate and seemingly unrelated symptoms, and they may feel less guilty for having depression and its associated decrements in functioning when this occurs. While cognitive therapy (CT; Beck, Rush, Shaw, & Emery, 1979) asks clients to identify and explore dysfunctional thoughts and to try behavioral experiments, IPT asks clients to try experiments that are interpersonal in nature, based on what they have identified as dysfunctional in their social roles and interpersonal relationships. Although both can be successful for individuals with depression, IPT targets the interpersonal challenges that are universal to most, if not all, individuals in resolving depression. IPT may also be an effective alternative to CT when clients have difficulty identifying or resolving dysfunctional thoughts. The interpersonal target provides them with another focus of therapeutic work, especially when focusing on thoughts seems more difficult. Although IPT was originally developed for the treatment of depression, the components that make it such a successful treatment are also applicable to a number of other disorders. Thus, it may be used to treat other psychological challenges quite effectively.

UNIQUE ASPECTS OF IPT

When Gerald L. Klerman, Myrna M. Weissman, and their collaborators embarked on the New Haven-Boston Collaborative Research Project in the 1960s, the research project out of which IPT was created, they likely did not know the profound impact that their work would have on the treatment of individuals with major depression and other disorders. Now, roughly 40 years later, the influence of the treatment that emerged out of that study is almost certainly far broader than they could have imagined as they were conceiving that original study. IPT has developed as an effective treatment for individuals who experience depression at many stages of the life span, and it has been successfully adapted for use with clients experiencing a wide variety of disorders (e.g., Hollon et al., 2005; Lipsitz et al., 2006; Schulberg, Scott, Madonia, & Imber, 1993). Moreover, the use and popularity of IPT has spread around the globe to communities in Europe, South America, and Africa. In recent years, s IPT has been effectively implemented with clients from widely varied backgrounds and by non-Western clinicians in non-Western cultures. The fact that IPT has reached and been found beneficial in so many communities speaks to Klerman and Weissman's ability to envision a treatment that appears to have near-universal applicability.

The characteristics of IPT that make it unique among the empirically supported treatments are likely also related to its popularity and ease of use among clinicians and its acceptance and effectiveness among clients. IPT is a treatment that "makes sense," both to the clinicians implementing it and to their clients. Because it focuses on universal human problems, clients seem to intuitively understand and accept the fact that significant stresses in their lives contribute to changes in their mood and other symptoms of distress. Likewise, it is logical for clinicians to focus therapeutic work on interpersonal relationships, particularly because therapy itself is so interpersonal in nature. The applicability of IPT to such a large portion of the client population is likely based on the fact that the theory underlying the treatment rests on challenges that most, if not all, individuals face at some point in their lives: problems in interpersonal relationships and adapting to new social roles. IPT is applicable to even those individuals who are lacking in social contacts, as the treatment focus can also be on this particular form of interpersonal dysfunction. Although individuals may differ in the extent to which they face social difficulties, some such challenges confront all of us at some point in our lives; IPT appeals on the basis of this universality.

IPT may also be beneficial because it arms clients with resources for dealing with interpersonal difficulties that may arise in the future, even after treatment has ceased. IPT encourages clients to become and to remain active in improving their situations under the guidance of an experienced therapist. The fact that IPT may also be implemented successfully in conjunction with pharmacotherapy allows clients who require the addition of medication to reap the benefits of both treatments (Klerman et al., 1984; Weissman et al., 2000). Moreover, the short-term nature of IPT provides an effective treatment option for clients whose financial situation or other responsibilities only allow for a finite number of sessions.

What follows in this work is a brief description of the history of IPT, a detailed explanation of the format of the treatment, the specific strategies used in IPT, and a thorough review of the research findings demonstrating the value of the treatment. We have been purposeful in including descriptions of IPT modifications and evidence as to the success of IPT with a variety of client populations and disorders. As will be evident, the research on IPT has demonstrated that it has broad relevance to a wide range of clinical challenges, and the list is still growing. A list of resources for clinicians is provided, as well as a description of current developments and new directions for IPT.

2

History

This chapter discusses the development of interpersonal psychotherapy (IPT). Its unique historical origin within the context of a research setting is described, as well as the theories in which IPT is based. The history of the development and dissemination of IPT and its evolution within the context of a treatment trial are discussed. Finally, recent work adapting IPT and testing the efficacy of these adaptations is reviewed.

ORIGINS

Although the description of many therapeutic modalities typically begins with a discussion of the theoretical basis of the treatment, ours begins with an account of an empirical study, as IPT actually developed within a research setting. Of course, IPT has roots in the theories of the interpersonal school of psychology and psychiatry, which will be described. However, given the distinctive origins of this treatment, we begin with a description of its evolution as it actually occurred. Interested readers can reference Myrna Weissman's (2006) work, which recounts this history in more detail.

Portions of this chapter have been adapted from "Interpersonal Psychotherapy," by C. L. Cornes and E. Frank, 1996, in L. J. Dickstein, J. M. Oldham, and M. B. Riba (Eds.), *Review of Psychiatry*, pp. 91–108. Copyright 1996 by American Psychiatric Association. Adapted with permission.

The original development of IPT was initiated by Gerald L. Klerman, Myrna M. Weissman, and collaborators in the late 1960s within the research setting of the New Haven-Boston Collaborative Research Project. The project aimed to "test the relative efficacy of a tricyclic antidepressant alone and both with and without psychotherapy as a maintenance treatment of ambulatory nonbipolar depression" (Weissman, 2006, p. 553). This treatment trial was focused specifically on preventing relapse among individuals who had recently recovered from depression. While the overall purpose of the trial was to improve treatment and prevent recurrence of major depression, a significant and novel component of this goal was to conduct a clinical trial in which all of the therapists were providing a standardized treatment. The resolution of any research group to provide the same treatment to all study participants was a relatively new practice for a treatment trial at this time, which set IPT apart as a progressive treatment for depression.

Psychiatric work in the historical context of the late 1960s and early 1970s meant that most psychiatric research focused on psychopharmacology. Psychotherapeutic treatments that were used were typically psychodynamic, although the development of Beck's cognitive therapy was occurring simultaneously (Weissman, 2006). One of Klerman's goals was to design a study that imitated true clinical practice as much as possible. Most patients in treatment in clinical practice were receiving both psychotherapy and pharmacotherapy; thus, the maintenance treatment trial planned to include psychotherapy in addition to medication. However, as Weissman (2006) describes, it was not the researchers' initial intention to develop IPT as a treatment for depression, as it was not yet clear at the time whether psychotherapy had a role in relapse prevention. For both of these reasons, psychotherapy was included in the trial, even "if for nothing more than a milieu effect" (Weissman, 2006, p. 554).

When designing the psychotherapy for this trial, the researchers were looking to include a psychotherapy condition considered a supportive treatment that was short enough to match the time-limited nature of the depression treatment planned for the maintenance trial (Klerman & Weissman, 1993; Weissman, 2006). Within the research project, this goal was accomplished by adopting the strategies of experienced social workers, which may have been new to academic psychiatry given the emphasis on psychodynamic psychotherapy at the time. The psychotherapy also built upon the interpersonal theories of Sullivan, Meyer, and Bowlby, as well as work on the role of life events (Weissman, 2006). Bowlby was invited to visit this group so that they could learn more about his ideas; the research group also spent time reading the works of these theorists and trying out specific therapeutic strategies with cases before writing the manual for the maintenance study, which was later conducted with National Institute of Mental Health (NIMH) funding (M. Weissman, personal communication, September 30, 2009).

When the findings of this maintenance study indicated that the psychotherapy was effective, Klerman, Weissman, and their colleagues decided to capitalize on its value by further developing and then testing a formal treatment that reflected the strengths of the psychotherapeutic approach used in their maintenance study. They observed the nature of the interpersonal relationships of the individuals in their maintenance study, which, along with regular reports from study therapists and the original treatment manual, were used to guide the development of the formal treatment. They called it interpersonal psychotherapy and designed an acute treatment study of pharmacotherapy alone, IPT alone, and their combination to more formally test the efficacy of IPT (Weissman, 2006).

After IPT was shown to be effective in two clinical trials, Klerman and Weissman's group published a manual outlining the theoretical orientation of the interpersonal approach and the set of strategies that had since evolved into IPT (Klerman et al., 1984). The treatment integrated aspects of cognitive, behavioral, psychodynamic, and supportive techniques (Rockland, 1992). Some of the psychotherapeutic strategies involved included expression of affect from psychodynamic psychotherapy, behavioral activation from cognitive therapy, and a positive therapist stance from supportive therapy. Communication analysis is also used, a technique that was later also incorporated into family-focused treatment for the treatment of families in which one member suffers from bipolar disorder or schizophrenia (Miklowitz, 2008; Miklowitz & Goldstein, 1997). Since this time, IPT has garnered strong empirical support as a treatment for depression (e.g., Blom et al., 2007; Elkin et al., 1989; Frank et al., 1990; Frank, Kupfer, Wagner,

McEachran, & Cornes, 1991; Klerman & Weissman, 1987; Markowitz & Weissman, 2004; Reynolds et al., 1999; Weissman & Markowitz, 1994).

THEORETICAL ORIGINS

As mentioned above, the originators of IPT were influenced by several theorists in developing this approach. The treatment is based in the interpersonal school of psychology and psychiatry, a school of thought in the area of mental health that first appeared in the 1930s and 1940s (Klerman et al., 1984). This work was based in the Washington–Baltimore area and primarily included theories of Harry Stack Sullivan and the neo-Freudians, Frieda Fromm-Reichmann, Erich Fromm, and Karen Horney. Most notably, the interpersonal school differentiated itself from others by its emphasis on the importance of social roles and an individual's closest relationships (Klerman et al., 1984). The originators of IPT emphasized the link between interpersonal dysfunction and psychopathology in creating IPT; they used the ideas of these notable theorists to develop methods of ameliorating symptoms by resolving social challenges. This conceptualization focused on life events that occur in a social context and the concept of the human as a fundamentally social being. The techniques used in IPT today are founded on these ideas.

However, we can also see how current use of IPT reflects the therapy's origins in a research context. The use of IPT as a treatment for depression, especially early on, was related to the development of the treatment in the original maintenance study of depression. Numerous modifications of IPT have been developed for other populations and disorders, but these did not come about until 10 to 15 years after IPT originated. Publications describing the use of IPT in the NIMH Treatment of Depression Collaborative Research Program (TDCRP) in the late 1980s and early 1990s put IPT on the map as an effective treatment for depression, and perhaps one that could be adapted to treat other disorders. The active and directive stance of the therapist, to be described later in more detail, also relates to the early beginnings of IPT in a research context. As a time-limited treatment, therapists actively focus the client's attention on the important aspects of treatment, naturally leading them to use a more directive stance than might be seen in other modalities.

HISTORY OF THE DEVELOPMENT
AND DISSEMINATION OF IPT

Although IPT has successfully managed to make its way into multiple research studies that demonstrate its success, as well as into a small but growing number of routine clinical settings, it is unfortunate that it has taken almost 40 years for the popularity of this treatment to reach mainstream psychology. Over these 40 years, IPT has become known to researchers and clinicians via a variety of routes.

Drs. Klerman and Weissman and their group at New Haven developed the initial precursor to IPT for a maintenance treatment study of depression and subsequently conducted a study of this treatment in an acute treatment setting (DiMascio et al., 1979; Klerman, DiMascio, Weissman, Prusoff, & Paykel, 1974; Weissman, Klerman, Paykel, Prusoff, & Hanson, 1974). Following this work, two other studies helped with the diffusion of IPT within the United States: the NIMH TDCRP and the Pittsburgh study of Maintenance Therapies in Recurrent Depression (MTRD). The NIMH TDCRP (Elkin et al., 1989) involved the training of research clinicians at three centers (George Washington University, University of Pittsburgh, and University of Oklahoma). The training of clinicians for this study was conducted by Gerald Klerman, Myrna Weissman, Bruce Rounsaville, and Eve Chevron, who were the authors of the original IPT manual (Klerman et al., 1984). The MTRD study (Frank et al., 1990) involved the training of a separate group of research clinicians at the University of Pittsburgh, also by Klerman, Weissman, Rounsaville, and Chevron. Many of the research clinicians involved in these two studies, in turn, began training other clinicians, first in their home universities and then at other centers within the United States and Canada. Some of these "second- and third-generation" clinicians have now gone on to establish their own centers for training in IPT, from which trainees may take IPT with them to professional careers as researchers and clinicians. Although by 2004, compared to Beck and colleagues' cognitive therapy (Beck et al., 1979), relatively few training programs had made IPT part of their psychiatric residency or clinical psychology curriculum (Weissman et al., 2006), the number is increasing.

In addition to this diffusion stream, an important source of IPT dissemination has been the young people—particularly John Markowitz and Laura Mufson—who Gerald Klerman trained once he left his post as director of the Alcohol, Drug Abuse and Mental Health Administration and came to Cornell University. Mufson's first work on IPT was conducted when she was a postdoctoral fellow, under the mentorship of Myrna Weissman. Both Markowitz and Mufson subsequently conducted important research studies of IPT, and Markowitz especially has been invited to conduct IPT training seminars throughout Europe and North America. Laura Gillies at Toronto and, later, Paula Ravitz and her group have also been an important source of IPT dissemination in both the United States and Canada.

In Europe, IPT spread to Germany principally following the training of one English-speaking German clinician, Elisabeth Schramm, who spent a year learning IPT in Pittsburgh. She, in turn, has been responsible for multiple training courses in Germany and in the conduct of IPT research there. Giuseppe Berti Ceroni of the University of Bologna aided in the dissemination of IPT in Italy. After learning IPT from Myrna Weissman, he conducted IPT trainings in Italy and translated the original IPT manual into Italian. The adoption of IPT in Italy was also greatly helped by one essentially self-taught clinician, Paolo Scocco of Padua, who initially sought consultation with the Pittsburgh group and then went on to train research clinicians and, later, community clinicians there. IPT translations in books also exist in German, French, Japanese, Danish, and Spanish, and a Portuguese version is underway.

The influence of IPT in Europe also increased as a result of several workshops conducted by John Markowitz in the 1990s, including trainings in Scandinavia, the Netherlands, Switzerland, Italy, Germany, and the United Kingdom. His training in the United Kingdom in 1998 included collaboration with Elizabeth and Stephen Martin at Durham. Laurie Gillies of the Toronto group was also conducting IPT trainings in Leicester around the same time.

Marc Blom and his research group in the Netherlands began working with IPT in 1990 after a colleague had attended a workshop lead by Gerald Klerman and brought IPT back to their group. After conducting a small pilot of IPT with depressed outpatients, Dr. Blom attended a workshop led by John Markowitz in 1992, where he received formal training in IPT. After receiving supervision by Kathleen Clougherty and attending subsequent trainings with John Markowitz and Scott Stuart, Dr. Blom began giving courses in IPT for Dutch therapists. The Dutch Society for IPT has since been established, with 36 IPT supervisors and hundreds of trained therapists in the country. Blom's group has since conducted a study on the efficacy of IPT (e.g., Blom et al., 2007).

In Australia and New Zealand, the dissemination of IPT was largely supported by trainings conducted there by Myrna Weissman and John Markowitz. Dr. Markowitz taught IPT in these countries in the late 1990s, at which time Sue Luty's group was working on an adaptation of IPT for anorexia nervosa in Christchurch, New Zealand, to be discussed in a later chapter. IPT has also spread to South America, primarily with the work of Marcelo Feijo de Mello, who has conducted studies on IPT for chronic depression in Brazil (de Mello, Myczcowisk, & Menezes, 2001).

IPT has been implemented in Japan by Hiroko Mizushima, a psychiatrist and former member of the Japanese parliament. She began work on IPT in the 1990s after attending workshops lead by Drs. Weissman and Mufson in Japan. Dr. Mizushima increased the availability of IPT in Japan by translating some IPT manuals into Japanese (translations of Klerman et al., 1984; Weissman et al., 2000; Weissman et al., 2007; Wilfley, Mackenzie, Welch, Ayres, & Weissman, 2000), by writing review articles on IPT in Japanese journals, by speaking about IPT at academic societies, and by leading regular introductory training workshops and monthly group supervision. IPT has also become known to Japanese laypeople and consumers through self-help IPT books written by Dr. Mizushima. A study of psychotherapy efficacy by Dr. Mizushima's group, sponsored by the Japanese Ministry of Health, Welfare, and Labor Policies, is currently underway.

The spread of IPT to sub-Saharan Africa first came about as a result of a World Health Organization (WHO) research study (Bolton et al., 2003; Verdeli et al., 2003), for which two clinicians from the Cornell-Columbia group, Kathleen Clougherty and Helena Verdeli, provided the initial training to indigenous health workers. More recently, the Toronto Addis Ababa Psychiatric Project (TAAPP; Alem, Pain, Araya, & Hodges, in press), in which University of Toronto faculty have helped to build a sustainable psychiatric training program at Addis Ababa University in Ethiopia, has included two blocks of IPT training courses taught by Paula Ravitz in 2006 and 2008. Psychiatry residents who went on to become faculty and clinical staff were trained in IPT and thus form a nucleus of potential trainers. The TAAPP IPT training focused on skills-based teaching of IPT guidelines and clinical techniques adapted to be more feasibly implemented in local mental health settings, to be acceptable and of relevance to Ethiopian culture, and to address life stressors of individuals living there (Weissman et al., 2007). In addition, new IPT developments are currently underway in Congo, Goa, Greece, and China.

Another factor in the spread of IPT has been the organizing of the International Society of Interpersonal Psychotherapists (ISIPT), which held its first meeting in Pittsburgh in June 2004. This meeting was followed by a second international conference in Toronto in November 2006 and a third international conference in New York City in March 2009. At the most recent meeting, presentations described the use of IPT and IPT adaptations in Japan and India, in addition to many of the countries listed above. The ISIPT now maintains a membership list and a website that aids communication among those interested in IPT.

RECENT HISTORY

Building on the initial work of the developers of IPT and early studies demonstrating the feasibility and efficacy of the treatment, the recent history of IPT has highlighted the therapy's acceptability and value in a variety of contexts and cultures, as outlined above. Recent work has also explored the utility of IPT as compared to additional treatment strategies, both for depression and for the treatment of a number of other disorders. These developments will be outlined here.

As with the early use of IPT, noted in the previous section, historically, much of the research on the feasibility and efficacy of IPT has been carried out in North America or Western Europe (e.g., Elkin et al., 1989; Miller, Gur, Shanok, & Weissman, 2008; Mufson et al., 1994). Although these studies have explored the use of IPT in the industrialized, Western culture where it was developed, as IPT has spread to other parts of the world, recent work has focused on modifying IPT for the treatment of other disorders and for populations that differ from the client group on whom the therapy was initially tested.

In one such recent project, Verdeli's group (2003) tested a modified version of group IPT for depressed individuals in rural Uganda (Group IPT in Rural Uganda, IPT-GU), part of the WHO-sponsored research study described in the previous section. The modifications accounted for the changes necessitated by cultural, socioeconomic, and lifestyle differences among this population, such as the devastation of the human immunodeficiency virus (HIV) in this part of the world. The treatment was modified by targeting symptoms more relevant to this group's culture, facilitating disclosure, increasing the flexibility of the treatment structure, and modifying the various foci of treatment to be more meaningful to this group (Verdeli et al., 2003). The problem areas of treatment focus the client's work on one or two areas, including grief, role transitions, role disputes, and interpersonal deficits. These will be discussed in more detail in Chapter 3.

The efficacy of IPT-GU is discussed in more detail in Chapter 5, in which we review how IPT works with diverse clients. Also in this section, we discuss in detail the use of IPT in rural mental health centers, as IPT has been identified as potentially effective for depressed adolescents seeking treatment at these venues (Bearsley-Smith et al., 2007). Recent research has also shown that adaptations of IPT may be used effectively in a variety of cultures, such as when used for depressed clients in Italy (Bellino, Zizza, Rinaldi, & Bogetto, 2007) and for individuals with dysthymia (IPT-D; Markowitz, 1996; Markowitz, 1998) in Brazil (de Mello et al., 2001). All of these recent adaptations highlight the application of IPT to diverse settings.

Work in recent decades has also focused on modifying IPT for other psychological disorders. These include interpersonal and social rhythm therapy (IPSRT; Frank, 2005) for bipolar disorder and IPT for the treatment of comorbid panic symptoms (IPT-PS; Cyranowski et al., 2005) and social phobia (IPT-SP; Lipsitz et al., 2008). IPT has also been altered for the treatment of postpartum depression (Stuart & O'Hara, 1995) and eating disorders (e.g., Jones, Peveler, Hope, & Fairburn, 1993), among numerous other adaptations. These versions of IPT, to be described in Chapter 5, have demonstrated success at treating the clients they target.

Their importance, however, lies in the relevance of the core themes of IPT to these varied populations.

In recent years, there has also been a growing interest in identifying the most effective, long-lasting, and cost-effective treatment *strategies* involving psychotherapy and pharmacotherapy. In an effort to contribute to this area, our group compared sequential and combination treatment for recurrent depression (Frank, Grochocinski, et al., 2000). Women were treated with IPT and pharmacotherapy, given sequentially or in combination, during acute and maintenance phases of two trials. Despite a few limitations, the results showed that clients in the sequential treatment strategy demonstrated a higher rate of remission than those in combination treatment. Sequential treatment was somewhat slower in its onset, but is identified as less costly (Frank, Grochocinski, et al., 2000). This strategy provides an option for clients who cannot, or perhaps choose not to, maintain treatment with chronic pharmacotherapy.

Another analysis showed that more frequent sessions of maintenance IPT (weekly or biweekly) were no more effective at preventing recurrences than monthly IPT-M (Frank et al., 2007). This strategy may be valuable in reducing treatment cost by limiting the number of IPT-M sessions needed to maintain remission.

Overall, the importance of these maintenance studies is in their contribution to the identification and implementation of the best treatment and the best treatment strategy for each client. While past work demonstrating the utility of IPT is vital to the dissemination of an effective psychotherapy for a variety of clients, the recent work described here expands on early work by guiding treatment selection based on the needs of the client. Minimizing the costs of treatment while maximizing its (i.e., the treatments) efficacy has become a key focus of treatment outcome research in recent years, and this work contributes to our knowledge of the best implementation of IPT and pharmacotherapy.

This chapter has illustrated the unique historical origins of IPT and how this early work has contributed to its current use. Next, we discuss the theory behind IPT in more detail and review some unique features of this treatment.

3

Theory

This chapter aims to provide a general introduction to the treatment approach using interpersonal psychotherapy (IPT). It begins with a discussion of the theoretical basis of IPT and its evolution to the present, based on the work of other scientists. The goals of IPT are then described, along with a description of how these goals are achieved in treatment. Key IPT concepts are explained throughout the chapter.

EVOLUTION TO PRESENT/THEORETICAL BASIS OF IPT

Examining the psychological theories that shaped the nature of IPT, we find that IPT was based, in part, on Adolf Meyer's influential work in the interpersonal school of psychiatry, done mostly in the early to mid-1900s

Portions of this chapter have been reprinted and adapted from "Interpersonal Psychotherapy," by C. L. Cornes and E. Frank, 1996, in L. J. Dickstein, J. M. Oldham, & M. B. Riba (Eds.), *Review of Psychiatry, 15*, pp. 91–108. Copyright 1996 by the American Psychiatric Association. Adapted with permission; and "Interpersonal Psychotherapy for Unipolar and Bipolar Disorders," by H. A. Swartz, J. C. Markowitz, and E. Frank, 2002, in S. Hoffmann & M. Tompson (Eds.), *Treating Chronic and Severe Mental Disorders: A Handbook of Empirically Supported Interventions* (pp. 131–158). Copyright 2002 by Guilford Press. Reprinted with permission.

(Klerman et al., 1984). A supporter of the psychobiological approach, Meyer emphasized an individual's progress through the developmental stages and everyday demands of life to gain an understanding of his or her psychopathology (Meyer, 1957). Meyer was interested in the social relations and psychosocial features of an individual's environment, and he focused on these factors in his approach to human behavior and psychiatry. As such, he theorized that a person's psychopathology was the result of the individual's attempt to deal with the psychosocial environment, which laid the groundwork for theories on the importance of the interpersonal environment in an individual's pathological behavior (Klerman et al., 1984).

Meyer's (1957) psychobiological approach to human behavior focused strongly on "psychology based on practical demands" and less on abstract psychology or psychiatry (p. 45). He was interested in pragmatic, commonsense psychotherapy and, as such, wanted to explore human socialization, the way we interact with each other day to day (Meyer, 1957). Meyer emphasized the psychosocial features of an individual's environment; he defined mental illness as "an attempt by the individual to adapt to the changing environment" (Klerman et al., 1984, p. 42). Moreover, Meyer emphasized the current experiences and social relations of the individual with regard to his theory of psychiatry.

Harry Stack Sullivan, another contributor to the interpersonal school of psychiatry, was greatly influenced by Adolf Meyer's theories. Sullivan viewed psychiatry as having a strong relationship to the field of interpersonal relations, identifying the presence of "an acute need for a discipline which was determined to study . . . the interpersonal situations through which persons manifest mental health or mental disorder" (Sullivan, 1953, p.18). Based on this definition, Sullivan felt that psychiatry should focus on the study of people and the interactions between them, rather than the brain or the mind (Klerman et al., 1984). Moreover, the interpersonal school of psychiatry argued that if psychopathology is present, it may be a consequence of interpersonal dysfunction, although the opposite may also be true. The foundation of IPT addresses this concern, with the argument that improving the client's current interpersonal situation may change his or her experience with psychopathology. Likewise, when psychopathology has been reduced, interpersonal relationships may improve as a result.

Sullivan also used a developmental approach to describe how humans change through the influence of others by expanding upon Meyer's ideas on the effects of childhood interpersonal experiences. One way that Sullivan provided additional support for this theory of psychiatry was by study-ing the development of anxiety in an infant. In one particularly salient example, Sullivan explained that an infant will exhibit anxiety or disturbed behavior when his or her mother, or another significant other with whom the infant is interacting, has an "emotional disturbance" (Sullivan, 1953, p. 9). Sullivan points out that it is the anxiety in the significant other that induces anxiety in the infant, which perhaps we could understand as a learned response that occurs in a social context, rather than as an innate response to a stressor. Thus, Sullivan further supports his theory of the development of psychopathology in an interpersonal context.

The work of Frieda Fromm-Reichmann and Mabel Blake Cohen (Cohen, Baker, Cohen, Fromm-Reichmann, & Weigert, 1954) also focused on early experiences in understanding how early family life is reflected in the personality and interpersonal problems of individuals with bipolar disorder (Klerman et al., 1984). Again, the authors make the link between interpersonal experiences and later functioning. This evidence, with the work of Meyer and Sullivan reviewed here, provides support for the con-ceptual underpinnings of IPT as being strongly rooted in the interpersonal school of psychiatry, as laid out by Klerman and colleagues (1984).

Note that the use of the term *interpersonal school of psychiatry* here, rather than psychology or psychotherapy, is twofold. First, this term accu-rately reflects work in this area that was being conducted in the 1950s and 1960s; its proponents were mostly psychiatrists, who were trained as physi-cians and who applied their work on interpersonal style to their knowledge of psychiatry. Second, Gerald L. Klerman, one of the originators of IPT, was a psychiatrist who used his knowledge of the schools of psychiatry, as well as the psychiatric research setting from which IPT grew, in shap-ing the development of IPT. While work in this area spread to schools of psychology, it began in a psychiatric setting.

SOCIAL SUPPORT AND LIFE EVENTS

Social support (or a lack thereof) and stressful life events have been found to play a role in the development of depressive episodes. While Brown and Harris (1978) are clear in stating that life events and a lack of social support do not cause depression, their work and that of others (e.g., Henderson, Byrne, Duncan-Jones, Scott, & Adcock, 1980) argue for a strong connection between dysfunctional social relationships and the development of depression (Klerman et al., 1984). They state that this connection is most problematic for individuals who have a specific vulnerability to developing depression. A discussion of these factors is included here as it is clear that the work of Brown and Harris laid a strong foundation for the development of IPT, a treatment that focuses on the connection among stressful life events, difficulties related to social support, and the development of depression (Klerman et al., 1984).

Brown and Harris (1978) defined a "provoking agent" as a factor that may produce depression, including "life events ... and ongoing difficulties that may or may not have begun with a discrete incident" (p. 47). They define "vulnerability factors" as other social factors that only increase the risk of depression when a provoking agent is also present. The authors explain that an example of a provoking agent might be the loss of one's job if this sudden loss produces depression. An example of a vulnerability factor might be the death of one's pet, which might cause reduced daily activity and involvement in a dog-walking group but is not significant enough to lead to depression in its own right. The authors argue that vulnerability factors are not likely to lead to the development of depression unless a provoking agent is also present, which, together, increase an individual's likelihood of developing depression.

With a stronger focus on the role of social support, Aneshensel and Stone (1982) tested the buffering model of social support, the idea that sufficient social support can buffer against the negative effects of stress (Dean & Lin, 1977; Dean, Lin, & Ensel, 1981; both as cited in Aneshensel & Stone, 1982). Based on 1,000 interviews, the authors found that life events, particularly losses, were associated with depressive symptoms, and a lack of social support may contribute to the development of depression. They explain that a lack of social support may have a negative influence because it may signify a lack of significant relationships or the individual may perceive that the existing relationships are not fulfilling. On the other hand, the presence of support may have a positive influence on mental health, perhaps alleviating some symptoms of depression.

This description of the work in the interpersonal school of psychiatry and in the areas of social support and life events provides a general sense of the theoretical background of IPT. Next, the goals and key concepts of IPT are presented and linked to this theoretical background.

GOALS

Interpersonal psychotherapy is a short-term, focused therapy that was initially created for the treatment of unipolar depression (Klerman et al., 1984). IPT focuses on the relationship between two factors: an individual's interpersonal relationships and social roles, particularly the difficulties within them, and the development or maintenance of depression. This relationship is one of the key concepts of IPT. The original manual of Klerman and colleagues (1984) explains that an underlying principle of IPT is that "disturbances in social roles can serve as antecedents for clinical psychopathology" (p. 48). Thus, a major tenet of IPT is that if the therapist and client can identify and improve the dysfunctional interpersonal strategies used by the client, they may be able to ameliorate the client's depression (Markowitz, Bleiberg, Christos, & Levitan, 2006).

It is most important for the client to understand the link between interpersonal difficulties and depression to conduct successful work in IPT. This link is the basis for therapeutic work and change and provides a rationale for the client to engage in emotional processing and behavioral modifications. The therapist can use the information gained in the "interpersonal inventory" that he or she conducts at the outset of treatment to connect changes in social roles to depression in a way that is meaningful to the client. The therapist helps the client to identify and effectively prepare for future changes in social roles, to improve current interpersonal relationships and communication, and to identify interpersonal difficulties that may arise in the future. Throughout the course of treatment, the therapist arms the client with resources to aid him or her in more adaptively coping with these challenges in the present and the future. However, these strategies cannot be used effectively unless the connection between interpersonal challenges and affective symptoms is made clear.

The interpersonal approach to therapy outlined in Klerman and colleagues' (1984) manual views depression as made of three component processes: symptom formation, social and interpersonal relations, and personality patterns. However, the goals of IPT relate solely to the first two processes. The third is not addressed because the "relatively brief duration and low level of psychotherapeutic intensity" of the treatment is not expected to have a major impact on personality (Weissman et al., 2000, p. 8). Nonetheless, some individuals demonstrate a lessening of personality difficulties by the end of treatment (Cyranowski et al., 2004). IPT rests on the assumption that the focus of therapy is on the client's current symptoms and interpersonal experiences. As we will see, this is important in the formation of the goals of IPT.

Therapeutic Goals

The first goal is to begin to reduce the client's depressive symptoms by educating the client about his or her current experience. The therapist helps to place the client's current symptoms in the context of major depression and describes depression as a common disorder that is well understood by mental health professionals and is quite treatable. This psychoeducation is another key concept of IPT. Some clients, especially those experiencing their first episode of depression, may not have a name for the symptoms they are reporting nor an understanding of what the illness involves. The therapist identifies the client's decrements in functioning and vegetative signs as aspects of depression, rather than the client's laziness or a failure, as is often assumed by those with the disorder. The therapist is careful to describe the typical course of the disorder, noting that with some effort on the part of the client and assistance from the therapist, depression is a treatable disorder from which the client is likely to recover.

The second goal, related to the focus on the client's current interpersonal relationships, is to help the client understand the means by which he or she deals with relationships and interpersonal conflicts. Often, a client is not able to identify the adaptive or maladaptive strategies he or she uses in interpersonal interactions. Thus, when problems arise, a client may be taken by surprise and may not readily identify the underlying cause of the difficulty, as well as its relationship to the development of depression. By identifying his or her methods, the client will gain a more thorough knowledge of each strategy's effectiveness or lack thereof and will understand more completely how to form healthy relationships and resolve interpersonal conflicts. Thus, the underlying premise of IPT previously described reinforces the idea that the overall goal of treatment, the amelioration of depressive symptoms, is achieved via the secondary goal of improving the interpersonal functioning relationships of the client. Improved interpersonal relationships may play a role in the prevention of future depressive episodes and may also provide more pleasant and adaptive social experiences.

Childhood Experiences

IPT acknowledges the significant effect of childhood experiences on the formation of later relationships, with the idea that these past social bonds should "enhance understanding of the patient's pattern of interpersonal relationships" (Weissman et al., 2000). The attention to childhood experiences is not a goal of IPT, per se, but it does reflect the overall viewpoint of the treatment. While one might expect IPT to focus primarily on the client's early developmental events and intrapsychic defenses given their role in later relationships, this is typically not the case. Past relationships are seen as influencing how the client experiences current social situations, but IPT does not focus on these past relationships other than as a way of understanding current interpersonal difficulties (Weissman et al., 2000).

As a result of this strong emphasis on the client's *current* interpersonal relationships, a substantial amount of time is spent identifying the most significant people in the client's life and describing the relationships among them at the start of treatment. The identification and description of these relationships are termed the *interpersonal inventory* (Klerman et al., 1984; Weissman et al., 2000), which is another key concept of treatment. The therapist conducts the interpersonal inventory at the start of treatment by asking the client about his or her current significant relationships, as well as those that were important in the past. He or she will ask about the nature of the relationship, the duration, and the current status of the relationship, or if and how it ended. In addition to gathering information about the client's social contacts, this tool provides the basis of treatment conceptualization in which the therapist will link the client's depression to his or her interpersonal situation and will emphasize the importance of focusing on current social conflicts and stressors in treatment (Klerman et al., 1984; Weissman et al., 2000). The therapist uses this information to understand and more effectively treat present concerns, based on the viewpoint that information gained from past relationships and depressive episodes is best used as a way of understanding current interpersonal difficulties.

PROBLEM AREA FOCI

Within the formal structure of treatment, the therapist links the client's depression to an interpersonal disturbance by assigning the client's interpersonal difficulties to one of four problem areas: grief, role transitions, role disputes, or interpersonal deficits. This is perhaps the most specific and uniquely IPT concept. These problem areas were chosen based on a content analysis of what the early IPT therapists were naturally tending to focus on in treatment. It became apparent as IPT developed that the focus of treatment typically centered on these issues, concerns that are widely applicable to individuals with depression in a range of cultural and ethnic backgrounds.

Based on the information that the client provides in the interpersonal inventory, as well as his or her current symptoms and concerns, the therapist and client work together to agree on which of four problem areas (unresolved grief, role transitions, role disputes, interpersonal deficits) best addresses the client's current distress (Stuart & Robertson, 2003; Weissman et al., 2000). However, if disagreement between client and therapist occurs, Weissman and colleagues suggest it may be necessary and more productive to accept the client's treatment goals, at least temporarily. This is done in an effort to improve the therapeutic alliance at the beginning of therapy and as a way of quickly beginning treatment. Therapists can take comfort in the possibility that, at a later point, the treatment focus may shift to the problem area that the therapist had initially thought was the best fit for the client (Weissman et al., 2000).

Thus, the problem area focus may change in the course of therapy, and therapeutic work may focus on one or two problem areas (Weissman et al., 2000). In acute IPT treatment for depression, it is recommended that therapy focus on only one or two problem areas because of the short-term, focused nature of IPT. At times, in maintenance treatment, for example, multiple problem areas may be the focus as the therapy evolves and changes over a longer period of time. However, in acute treatment, honing in on one or two specific problems allows these issues to be developed more fully within the treatment sessions. Focusing on a different problem every week may simply serve to "put out fires" that the client brings in, but not to fully process any problem. Keeping a more or less relentless focus on one or, at most, two of these problem areas throughout treatment and not permitting the client–therapist dyad's attention to wander is, itself, a key concept of this short-term intervention. A full description of each problem area is provided in Chapter 4.

ADDITIONAL KEY CONCEPTS

While IPT does recommend the use of a number of specific strategies, a structured time format, and clear modifications of the treatment for different disorders, a number of key concepts guides treatment more broadly. Some of these have been noted in earlier sections of the chapter, including the link between interpersonal dysfunction and psychopathology and the use of interpersonal inventory. The remainder will be discussed here.

Medical Model and the Sick Role

One strategy is the use of the medical model—more specifically, the sick role (Klerman et al., 1984; Weissman et al., 2007). The medical model names the disease or disorder from which the client is suffering and identifies it as a treatable condition that is separate from the individual, not a reflection of his or her personality. The use of the medical model is based on the work of the IPT creators in medical settings. Moreover, some had backgrounds in medicine. However, the treatment was not (and is not now) mostly medically focused. Indeed, in creating IPT, Gerald Klerman was ahead of his time in understanding that psychological treatments could be appropriate for medical disorders. He grasped the importance of integrating psychological and medical care, the prescription of medications where appropriate, and the integration of the medical model more generally within the social, interpersonal framework of IPT.

Within the medical model, the therapist assigns the "sick role" to the client (Klerman et al., 1984; Weissman et al., 2007). Parsons (1951) created this concept, the purpose of which includes the client's exemption from some social obligations and responsibilities, his or her identification as a person who is in a socially undesirable emotional state and is in need of help, and the client's agreement to cooperate with the care provider to work toward getting well. Acceptance of the sick role may help to remove some of the stigma that still surrounds a diagnosis of depression.

Although some models of psychotherapy oppose the concept of the sick role, IPT embraces this role by identifying the illness and then separating it from the client's innate personality. When individuals are ill with other medical disorders, they are accorded a special status, given care, and relieved of some responsibilities. The analogy often used is that of diabetes; the therapist explains that if the client had diabetes, he or she would likely not hesitate to seek treatment, would make the appropriate lifestyle changes, and would take the treatments deemed necessary by a professional. Likewise, the therapist identifies depression as a disease that needs appropriate treatment, reinforcing the view of the client as a person with a medical illness. The use of the sick role may also strengthen the therapeutic relationship, which is important given the short-term nature of treatment.

The sick role may also be used when treating other disorders with IPT. For example, when treating bipolar disorder, a chronic illness, or an eating disorder, the sick role may help the client to accept the long-term or recurrent nature of the illness and to make accommodations based on limitations that may accompany the disorder.

As the sick role implies that the client likely suffers from a recurrent illness, the client may need time to grieve the lost healthy self, as described in the discussion of the grief problem area earlier in this chapter. This grief is different from the grief that is experienced over the loss of a loved one; here, the client works to identify himself or herself as a person with a psychiatric illness. The client will identify the pieces of the healthy self that he or she will be sad to lose and will talk about realistic changes that need to be made to accommodate the disorder. The purpose of this grieving process is to help facilitate the integration and acceptance of these accommodations and to give the client the confidence that he or she can maintain a full and happy life despite the disease.

The integration of the medical model as a core component of IPT may make it more likely that adjunctive pharmacotherapy will be accepted by a client receiving IPT than someone receiving another type of treatment. While the appropriate use of combined pharmacotherapy and psychotherapy is a key concept of IPT, it is not a strategy that is unique to this modality. Nonetheless, regarding mental disorders akin to other medical illnesses increases the chance that a client facing a number of psychological disorders will embrace the use of medications where indicated.

Stance of the Therapist

The stance of the therapist is also a key concept of IPT. As will be discussed in more detail below, the therapist takes an active, positive stance with the client. In training new IPT therapists, we often refer to this as the "cheerleader" role. The therapist does not offer unconditional positive regard as in Rogerian therapy, but does support and encourage the client as he or she makes positive changes, while placing the blame for the client's setbacks on the depression itself, not the client. The positive stance of the therapist also aids in the formation of the therapeutic alliance, usually enabling therapeutic work to progress more quickly and effectively.

Encouraging Expression of Affect

Another strategy used in IPT is expression of affect, a core component of the therapeutic process and a strategy that is instrumental in bringing about change in the client. As is the case in a variety of treatment modalities, some clients tend to repress or deny the painful feelings they have, and many may not have the opportunity to discuss their experiences and feelings with others outside of the therapy setting. Exploring, identifying, and processing feelings may offer these clients the opportunity to discuss painful emotions. Doing so is considered central to the curative process of IPT, as well as many other treatments. The catharsis that comes from expressing affect is based on the client's ability to recognize previously unknown feelings, to process these feelings, and to gain a greater understanding and insight into them.

A NOTE ON CULTURE

The problem areas discussed earlier in this chapter are one of the key features of IPT that make it a model that is universal to most, if not all, clients. In general, the link between social roles, interpersonal relationships, and mood that is central to the theory underlying IPT is a model that is easily understood and accepted by individuals in a variety of cultures. Moreover, IPT therapists, similar to therapists in any therapeutic modality, are sensitive to the culture and values from which the client originated and the cultures and values of the client's current environment. While the problem areas may need some slight adaptation for application to some cultures, as was done for the use of group IPT in Uganda, for example, the four treatment foci highlight interpersonal challenges faced by clients in almost all cultures and support the multicultural nature of IPT. Other adaptations to IPT are sometimes necessary when implementing the treatment in other cultures, but the link between interpersonal dysfunction and mood is generally accepted among a number of cultures worldwide.

This chapter has provided an explanation of how the theory underlying IPT is reflected in the treatment goals and the concepts that are of primary importance in this therapy. The next section will discuss how to achieve these goals and how the key concepts manifest in treatment. Case examples will be used to demonstrate the implementation of common techniques.

4

The Therapy Process

The purpose of this section is to provide a detailed understanding of how interpersonal psychotherapy (IPT) is conducted. First, the format of treatment is presented. A picture of the therapist–client relationship is then provided, and the therapist and client roles are described. We explain the key IPT strategies and how they are implemented in therapeutic work, and we also identify potential problems with the implementation of these strategies. Finally, we identify client populations for whom the use of IPT has been somewhat challenging and end with case examples highlighting these topics.

FORMAT OF TREATMENT, INITIAL PHASE

The format of IPT is closely linked to the goals of treatment and the concept of depression as directly related to interpersonal problems. We describe the format of treatment here, keeping in mind the treatment aims and the fact

Portions of this chapter have been reprinted and adapted from "Interpersonal Psychotherapy," by C. L. Cornes and E. Frank, 1996, in L. J. Dickstein, J. M. Oldham, & M. B. Riba (Eds.), *Review of Psychiatry*, 15, pp. 91–108. Copyright 1996 by American Psychiatric Association. Adapted with permission; and "Interpersonal Psychotherapy for Unipolar and Bipolar Disorders," by H. A. Swartz, J. C. Markowitz, and E. Frank, 2002, in S. Hoffmann and M. Tompson (Eds.), *Treating Chronic and Severe Mental Disorders: A Handbook of Empirically Supported Interventions* (pp. 131–158). Copyright 2002 by Guilford Press. Reprinted with permission.

that IPT is intended to be a short-term psychotherapy. Treatment in IPT usually lasts 16 to 20 sessions and is divided into three phases: an initial phase, which typically lasts 1 to 3 sessions, followed by a middle phase (roughly 10–14 sessions) and then a termination phase. The final 1 to 3 sessions typically constitute the termination phase. Therapists and clients usually meet once per week, with sessions lasting 45 to 60 minutes. Although IPT sessions are typically about 45 minutes in length, therapy sessions may run as long as 60 minutes when IPT and pharmacotherapy are used together. This additional time allows the therapist, and collaborating psychiatrist, if necessary, to review the client's symptoms and the side effects of the medication(s) that may be present, allows for the writing of prescriptions, and permits discussion of any medical concerns that have come up. It may not be possible for the client to be seen by a psychotherapist and collaborating psychiatrist in the same clinical setting, nor is it always necessary for the client to see a psychiatrist for pharmacotherapy if not clinically indicated.

Within the initial phase, the therapist and client begin with a review of the client's symptoms and the therapist's explanation of how depression will be treated with IPT. The therapist identifies and names the psychiatric symptoms the client is facing, normalizes the symptoms, and identifies them as part of depression or as limitations that may result from depressive symptoms. Presenting the sick role, the therapist and client then discuss the fact that it is not only normal but probably expected that the client cannot maintain his or her schedule of regular activities as would be done without the depression. Acceptance of this fact is explored and ways to deal with the guilt related to not maintaining normal activities are discussed. Accordingly, the client's need for medication is also assessed during the initial phase. Medication and IPT can be quite effectively used together, particularly with careful medication management under the guidance of a psychiatrist. Consulting with a psychiatrist and the use of medication, strategies that are not unique to IPT, are not only based on the background of the IPT creators and the use of the medical model, as described in Chapter 3, but also based on the fact that depression is often treated successfully with medication or a psychotherapy–medication combination. Of note, IPT allows, and even encourages, the use of medication when IPT is adapted for other disorders, as noted in the Chapter 3 discussion of key concepts.

The initial phase of treatment then moves on to the completion of the interpersonal inventory. As previously described, in addition to gaining information about the client's current and past relationships, this tool lays the groundwork for the therapist to link the client's depression to his or her interpersonal situation and to emphasize the importance of focusing on current social conflicts and stressors in treatment (Klerman et al., 1984; Weissman et al., 2000). Presumably, the therapist and client will uncover a social stressor that likely preceded the onset of the client's depression. While IPT does not aim to identify the cause (or causes) of a client's depressive episode, clients typically understand and accept the idea that the depression they experience is somehow related to a social stressor or interpersonal disturbance.

For example, a woman entered treatment after becoming depressed in the context of her children leaving for college. In the interpersonal inventory, the therapist's goal was to obtain a picture of the client's relationships and to use this information to relate the current episode to interpersonal dysfunction. The therapist began by asking about the most important people in the client's life, who were her husband, immediate family, and three or four close friends. The therapist inquired about the client's relationship with these individuals at present and what the relationships were like in the past. In particular, she was interested in the history and quality of these relationships, as well as the degree to which these relationships were reciprocated by the other party. The reason for this focus is to identify sources of social support or interpersonal difficulty that the client experiences in these relationships, as well as the pattern of social interaction the client has demonstrated in these relationships in the past. It appeared that the client had a moderately good network of social contacts, including family and close friends, but that she had trouble making use of their support and friendship when she was depressed. In addition, the client's relationship with her husband was generally good but strained at times, which had exacerbated her loneliness and depression since her children left for college. The strain in their relationship centered on disagreements pertaining to the number of hours per week that the client worked, and more generally to how soon the couple would begin retirement. While the client wanted to continue working, her husband preferred her to work fewer hours, and he wanted them to begin their retirement in the next couple of years.

The therapist also asked about past important relationships that the client had in order to learn about how the client navigated past interpersonal challenges and how she succeeded in maintaining relationships and garnering support from them in times of need. This information was used to give the therapist a picture of the client's general interpersonal functioning, in addition to identifying areas of strength and weakness in the client's social skills repertoire. The therapist also asked about interpersonal events that had occurred in the recent past, such as the departure of the client's two children for college one year and three years prior to the start of treatment, and the client reducing her work status to part time roughly five years prior. The client noted that reducing her work to part time was beneficial while her children were in high school so that she could spend additional time with them, but that she became lonely once her children left. The therapist used this information to link these recent interpersonal changes in the client's life to the development of her depressive symptoms. For example, with the therapist's guidance, the client could see that these challenging social changes, such as her children's leaving for college and arguing with her husband, have a direct effect on her mood. As the client had described how she dealt with changes in interpersonal relationships in the past, such as when a close coworker had moved to another company, the therapist used this information to plan effective treatment strategies that made use of the client's strengths. Using the information gained in the interpersonal inventory, the therapist and client planned to work on improving the client's current friendships, to increase her social contacts, and to create more regular and defined opportunities for social contact to improve her mood. They would also use communication analysis and role plays to improve communication with her husband.

As this example demonstrates, the therapist and client use information provided in the interpersonal inventory to choose a problem area focus of treatment that best relates to the client's current concerns. This collaborative process may be used to reflect back to the client the information that the therapist has received, as well as to reinforce the connection between interpersonal dysfunction and symptoms and to provide the client with a focus of treatment.

FORMAT OF TREATMENT, MIDDLE PHASE

A problem area of treatment (grief, role transitions, role disputes, interpersonal deficits) is identified by the start of the middle phase of treatment and may be amended during the middle phase as the client reveals more information about himself or herself. Once a primary problem area is identified, the client and therapist work collaboratively to improve the current interpersonal problem (Klerman et al., 1984). During the middle phase of treatment, the client and therapist delve deeper into the client's challenges, using some of the specific strategies outlined above, as well as some of the more general IPT techniques, to uncover and improve the dysfunctional nature of the client's interpersonal relationships. A lengthier description of the more general IPT techniques is provided later in this chapter. Briefly, these techniques include elicitation of detail, a focus on affect, communication analysis, decision analysis, and the use of behavioral activation, psychoeducation, and role plays. Symptoms are monitored every week, both to track the client's mood and to reinforce the connection between mood and the client's social situation. Moreover, as the therapeutic alliance increases during this phase, the therapist may use the therapeutic relationship as way for the client to practice the strategies learned for use in the client's other relationships. During this phase the identified problem area is the focus of treatment but may be discussed with regard to interpersonal concerns that arise from week to week. A description of each problem area follows.

Grief

Some individuals who suffer the loss of a loved one experience a grief reaction that is appropriate, both in severity and duration, given the seriousness of the loss; typically, these grief reactions do not lead to depressive episodes. For some individuals, however, the grief reaction is not resolved completely; for these individuals, it is possible that the lingering and unresolved feelings can be associated with the development of a depressive episode. In these cases, the grief problem area targets complicated grief or "abnormal grief reactions that result from failure to progress through the various phases of the normal mourning process" (Klerman et al., 1984, pp. 96–98; Weissman et al., 2007).

In his paper *Mourning and Melancholia* (Freud, 1917, as described in Cornes & Frank, 1996), Freud explained that grief reactions may be normal or abnormal. According to Freud, the normal grief process involves three parts: identifying and remembering previous events involving the deceased, experiencing feelings related to those memories, and slowly letting go of the past experiences while simultaneously moving toward new relationships and the development of a new life. Freud explained that this grieving process is more likely to lead to depression when the pain associated with the grief leads the individual to avoid experiencing important feelings, both positive and negative. So often in grief, the mourner has difficulty admitting the negative feelings that he or she has about the deceased, typically because of the guilt that accompanies the admission of these feelings. This avoidance of emotion hinders the resolution of ambivalent feelings regarding the lost person and may put individuals at risk for developing depression.

As such, the grief problem area aims to "facilitate the delayed mourning process" and later, to "help the client reestablish interests and relationships that can substitute for what has been lost" (Weissman et al., 2000, p. 64; Weissman et al., 2007). While some clients may find it easier to begin by resolving their ambivalent feelings before exploring new relationships, some clients find it just as therapeutic to begin establishing new contacts while still working on the metaphorical letting go of the lost loved one. The treatment strategies used in the grief problem area include exploration of the feelings associated with the loved one's death. During this process, it is imperative that the therapist positively reinforces the client for admitting to and expressing these feelings, with an emphasis on the fact that this will likely be a cathartic process for the client. Other strategies include thoroughly recalling and reconstructing important aspects of the past relationship; it is key for the depressed individual to remember not only the good parts of the past relationship, but also those that were less than ideal as a way of avoiding idealizing it (Weissman et al., 2007). This more balanced view of the relationship can lead to a fuller awareness of its past and present influence on the client's life. Finally, processing these thoughts and feelings can facilitate an increasing focus on improving existing relationships and developing new ones. Efforts toward new and existing relationships constitute the behavior change strategy used in the grief problem area. Of note, clients can also experience grief when identifying and accepting themselves as individuals with a mental illness. This grief process has a somewhat different focus than the grief problem area described here; it was discussed in Chapter 3.

Role Disputes

Individuals' social roles are based on the environment in which they live and work and the relationships they have. One woman's social roles may include wife, mother, executive, sister, and daughter. While the woman embodies each of these roles simultaneously, the behaviors and attitudes associated with each role may emerge more or less strongly based on the environment in which she is functioning. The roles are based on the individual's past and current interpersonal relationships, the environments in which he or she previously lived and worked, and the individual's attitudes regarding these roles. When the status of one's role is disputed, regardless of the reason, depression may result. For example, if a woman's job changes from part-time to full-time, she may expect her husband to help around the house as she no longer has as much time to devote to such activities. The husband and wife may disagree about the expectations each has of the husband's role in the housekeeping activities.

The role disputes problem area focuses on these nonreciprocal role expectations that exist between the client and her husband, or, in general, any other significant individual in a client's life with whom he or she has a role dispute (Klerman et al., 1984; Weissman et al., 2007). As the phrase implies, nonreciprocal role expectations include expectations that each party holds that are not shared by the other party to the dispute. Role disputes may be the result of such life events as job change, illness, aging, financial pressures, marriage, or welcoming a newborn. Klerman and colleagues (Klerman et al., 1984; Weissman et al., 2007) note that role disputes can lead to depression based on a feeling of lack of control in the dispute, repetitious disputes in which the client may feel stuck, or the feeling of hopelessness about the dispute, each of which can lead to reduced self-esteem. These factors, in turn, may contribute to depression.

Role disputes are characterized by weak communication patterns, feelings of discouragement, and, at times, the need to acknowledge that the differences may not be able to be resolved (Weissman et al., 2000). Each of these concerns surrounding the dispute needs to be addressed by the strategies used in this problem area, all of which fall within the more general goal of helping the client to "modify maladaptive communication patterns or reassess expectations" for the relevant relationship(s) (Klerman et al., 1984, p. 105; Weissman et al., 2007). Once a role dispute is recognized as the problem area of focus, the client and therapist need to identify the correct stage of the dispute: *renegotiation, impasse,* or *dissolution.* In the renegotiation stage, the client and his or her significant other are still actively working out their problems. This stage of a dispute may be characterized by more arguments and conflict than other stages, making the dispute actually appear worse. However, this is typical of the renegotiation stage, as the pair of individuals is still engaged in trying to repair the relationship; these attempts at repair may come in the form of arguments. During *impasse,* communication between the two parties, not to mention arguments between them, has ceased and has been replaced by feelings of anger and resentment. At this point, the client and his or her significant other try to determine whether the relationship is salvageable. Here, the therapist may use techniques to stir up discussion between the disputing parties. A relationship at the *dissolution* stage is characterized by irreconcilable differences and irreversible damage; at least one party to the dispute has decided that reconciliation is impossible and so the client must make efforts toward finding closure. At this stage, the therapist assists the client in ending the relationship, mourning feelings of loss for the old relationship, and developing new connections, similar to what is done in grief work.

Once the appropriate stage has been identified, the therapist and client devise a set of strategies for resolving the dispute or coming to terms with the dissolution of the relationship. The therapist encourages the client to evaluate his or her current expectations of the relationship and to negotiate new expectations with the other party to the dispute. As well, the therapist aids the client in the development of improved communication patterns and the modification of negative ones (Weissman et al., 2000). If the dispute has reached dissolution, the therapist assists the client in ending the relationship. In any of these stages, however, one of the therapist's major goals is to point out the connection between the existing nonreciprocal role expectations and the development and maintenance of both the dispute and the individual's depression. It is not uncommon in the role disputes problem area for the other party to the dispute to join the client and therapist for one or more sessions (Weissman et al., 2000). The purpose of these sessions is for the significant other to gain a greater understanding of the client's challenges, to increase a shared appreciation for both party's feelings and expectations within the relationship, and to improve communication between the individuals.

Role Transitions

As in the role disputes problem area, the role transitions problem area focuses on an individual's social roles; however, the treatment target here is the difficulty that a client may have when a change to a key social role occurs. In this problem area, the changes in these social roles contribute to the onset of the client's depression (Klerman et al., 1984; Weissman et al., 2007). Role transitions often occur as individuals traverse the developmental stages of life, typically accompanying such life events as marriage, a new job or a job change, moving, or having children.

For example, in the marital role transition, the client is adapting to the role of married person, while leaving behind part of his or her identity as a single person. Even when positive changes such as a marriage are occurring, apprehension or fear of the unknown may emerge; individuals often have difficulty coping with these feelings and transitions, potentially leading to depression. While some clients may have difficulty accepting the challenge that comes with adapting to this positive change, it is important that the therapist normalize the client's experience. The client should be reminded that, typically, these role transitions or life changes occur gradually over a period of time; allowing sufficient time to grieve the old role is a key piece of transitions work. Changes experienced as a loss can also be especially difficult to adapt to as they often lead to feelings of helplessness; as a result, depressive symptoms often emerge (Klerman et al., 1984), as well as impairment in social functioning. Often, the strategies used in role transitions that are experienced as a loss are similar to those used in grief work.

The therapist's major goal in the role transitions problem area is to help the client grieve the loss of the old role, to evaluate its past importance realistically (as opposed to in an unrealistically idealized manner), and to experience the emotions associated with giving it up. With the loss of an old role typically comes the emergence of a new role; here, the therapist's goal is to help the client evaluate the new role in an optimistic light and to identify positive features of this role (Weissman et al., 2000, 2007). In grieving the old role and welcoming the new one, the therapist will typically ask the client to describe the pieces of the old role that the client will miss, while also recounting the pieces that he or she will be glad to give up. Similarly, the client will be asked to describe the aspects of the new role that he or she will welcome, while acknowledging the parts that will not be as enjoyable. In this way, the client can obtain a realistic view of his or her feelings about the transition.

The therapist's final goal is to help the client increase feelings of self-confidence in the new and often unfamiliar setting of the acquired role by gaining new social contacts or learning new skills (Weissman et al., 2007). While also grieving the lost role, it is important for the client to test strategies for developing social supports in the context of the new role that he or she has discussed with the therapist. In addition, the therapist and client may brainstorm some ways in which the client may feel more competent in his or her new role; for example, an expectant mother may look into parenting classes, may begin to read books on welcoming a newborn, and may look to join a community group aimed at introducing new mothers. The new social skills, interpersonal contacts, and self-confidence gained through these efforts may not only improve the client's interpersonal situation but will hopefully have a positive impact on his or her mood.

Interpersonal Deficits

The interpersonal deficits problem area is assigned to those individuals with limited social contacts or inadequate, unsatisfying interpersonal relationships (Klerman et al., 1984; Weissman et al., 2007). These clients' lives are typically quite lonely, and they may feel isolated in their situation. While some of these clients may have never established intimate adult relationships, others may demonstrate difficulty in maintaining the existing attachments they have formed. In addition to the social isolation and dissatisfaction experienced by clients whose treatment focuses on interpersonal deficits, these individuals may have past depressive symptoms that have not been adequately resolved and that interfere with current relationships (Weissman et al., 2000). Naturally, these individuals' depressions tend to be more chronic than those in the other three problem areas, which can lead to interpersonal difficulties that persist over the long term.

For example, a man who has always found it somewhat difficult to connect with others may again find it difficult to develop social relationships with coworkers at his new job. While his coworkers include him in after-work social activities, the man's poor interpersonal skills make it challenging for him to form meaningful connections with his coworkers. Moreover, his chronic depression symptoms make it less likely that he will attend the activities, both because his energy is low and because his low self-esteem and anhedonia make it harder to attend when he does find the energy. Though he has good relationships with his close family members, he would like to develop other interpersonal relationships that are satisfying and lasting.

Based on these clients' characteristics and difficulties, the therapist's goals are to reduce the client's social isolation and dissatisfaction, to assist the client in forming new social contacts, and to help the client become more adept at maintaining them. In order to do so, the therapist begins by reviewing the positive and negative aspects of the client's current and past social relationships; if the client has few social contacts, the therapist may review characteristics of the client's relationships with family members. In this way, the interpersonal deficits problem area may focus on the client's interpersonal history to a greater extent than is typical of the other problem areas (Klerman et al., 1984). The purpose of this review is not only to get a thorough account of the client's current and past relationships, but also to evaluate these relationships as a way of identifying the common maladaptive patterns that are present in each (Weissman et al., 2007). The therapist will also look for patterns of interpersonal problems that arise in the therapeutic relationship to obtain direct information about how the client interacts with others; the therapist may inquire as to how the therapeutic relationship is analogous to other relationships in the client's life (Klerman et al., 1984; Weissman et al., 2007). Moreover, the therapist will help the client identify the positive aspects of his or her relationships that may be used to strengthen future social interactions.

It may take some time for the client to recognize the disadvantageous nature of his or her current and previous social strategies or the extent to which the client has remained isolated. The first step is for the therapist to help the client make these connections, as well as to understand how his or her interpersonal patterns are contributing to the depression. Based on the maladaptive patterns that the therapist may identify within the therapeutic relationship, the clinician may model for the client how to effectively develop and keep new and rewarding relationships (Klerman et al., 1984). The therapist will likely suggest that the client try out some experiments testing the new interpersonal strategies that the two have discussed and explore ways that the client can create some new social contacts. Most important, as with each of the problem areas of treatment, the therapist continues to make the connection between the client's current interpersonal situation and the development of the depression.

Choosing the Problem Area Focus

Undoubtedly, the problem area focus is one of the unique aspects of IPT, but choosing the problem area may require some attention. In general, the therapist and client will choose the problem area that involves the interpersonal problem most related to the onset of the depression. Knowing which problem area is most appropriate is based on information gained from the interpersonal inventory. On occasion, however, two interpersonal problems may be equally linked to the client's depression, or the client is not ready to focus on the problem area that the therapist feels would be most applicable. In this situation, it is advisable to let the client choose the problem area focus at the start of treatment. If the client initially avoids the problem area focus the therapist suggests, the client may become able to focus on this problem area after a good therapeutic alliance is established over the first few weeks of treatment.

FORMAT OF TREATMENT, FINAL PHASE

The final phase of treatment focuses on termination. Here, the therapist—and, it is hoped, the client as well—will acknowledge the reduction in the client's depressive symptoms that has occurred since the start of treatment. During this time, it is important for the two to review the symptoms of depression, especially those experienced by the client in the past, in order to prepare the client for the possibility of a recurrence that may arise after treatment has ended. However, the client is typically reminded that while recurrence is a possibility, he or she has made great gains and has acquired a vast array of tools while in therapy. The therapist and client also work on developing posttreatment coping strategies and assessing the need for continuation treatment (Klerman et al., 1984). The client and therapist may decide that continuing IPT in a maintenance format is advisable; this model of treatment will be discussed later. Also important during the termination phase is for the client to acknowledge and express the feelings he or she may have about ending treatment and leaving the therapist. At times, it is difficult for clients to do this, but as with all of phases of IPT, expression of affect is encouraged. Assessing the need for continued pharmacologic management may also be necessary.

THE THERAPIST–CLIENT RELATIONSHIP

The nature of the therapist–client relationship in IPT is one of structured roles, but it is also flexible and a reflection of the short-term duration of the treatment. Stuart and Robertson (2003) outline three underlying characteristics of the therapeutic relationship. First, they note that the relationship should have a high degree of affiliation, meaning that both parties have a genuine interest in and care for the other. Second, they note that the relationship should be inclusive, referring to the fact that working together should be important to both client and therapist. Finally, they emphasize the role of the therapist as an expert; this is not to say that the therapist commands the relationship without regard for the client's needs or desires while the client sits back passively. Rather, it is hoped that "the patient will view the therapist as having something of value to offer, and will be receptive to the therapist's feedback" (Stuart & Roberston, 2003, p. 161).

In a related way, the authors also note that it is the role of the therapist to establish the guidelines of therapy and to educate the client about the nature of IPT treatment (Stuart & Robertson, 2003). Of course, the therapist does not actually set and enforce "rules"; rather, he or she informs the client of the experience to be expected in IPT and perhaps provides some education about therapy in general, particularly if this is the client's first time in treatment. Likewise, it is expected that the client will adapt to treatment as laid out by the therapist and will communicate his or her needs or preferences within this general framework. This often occurs within the framework of the treatment contract. The contract set between the client and therapist not only lays out a few goals of treatment, such as to improve sleep hygiene or to improve communication with the client's sister, but also speaks to the logistical aspects of treatment, such as session frequency and duration (Weissman et al., 2000).

Overall, these aspects of the client–therapist relationship seem to be less influenced by the short-term nature of the treatment than other features of the treatment. Several facets of this relationship speak to the fundamental characteristics of IPT. For example, it is important, particularly for the therapist, to take timing into account when establishing an alliance with the client. Simply because there are typically 16 to 20 sessions in treatment using IPT, it is the therapist's responsibility to try to develop as strong a bond as possible with the client in a short amount of time. Similarly, the interpretation of transference is not included in IPT, in part based on the short-term nature of the treatment and in part based upon the underlying goals and tenets of IPT. With regard to the time-related concerns, Stuart and Robertson (2003) note that "the therapist must work actively and with intent in order to create and maintain a positive therapeutic alliance, and to prevent the development of problematic transference" (p. 162). There is also the sense that addressing the transference that could potentially arise within IPT could take up a number of sessions; the general rule of thumb in IPT is that while the client's reactions to the therapist are used to inform the therapist of the client's interpersonal style and social interactions with others, transference is not directly addressed in therapy (Stuart & Robertson, 2003).

However, IPT does not encourage therapists to completely discount problems that may arise in the therapeutic relationship but to view them slightly differently than might be done in a psychoanalytically based treatment. That is, the "here-and-now" focus of treatment encourages therapists to identify problematic interpersonal and communication patterns of the client in order to better understand how the client views the world and how he or she treats others (Weissman et al., 2000). Often, problems that arise in the therapeutic relationship fit into this category of interpersonal patterns, through which the therapist can gather valuable information about the client's relationship style (Stuart & Robertson, 2003). For example, a client who overestimates feeling unimportant to his friends may demonstrate this in session by rejecting or discounting the therapist's efforts to be empathic and offer help. Thus, the therapeutic relationship does not include analysis of transference, but it does promote the practical management of problems that arise in therapy as manifestations of challenges the client experiences in other social connections.

Finally, the therapeutic relationship in IPT is one of flexibility, collaboration, and individual variation. While the therapist may lay the groundwork for the format of treatment and may appear as the "expert" at times (Stuart & Robertson, 2003), the client and therapist are truly expected to work together toward the reduction of the client's symptoms and improvement of his or her well-being. This can be seen when choosing a problem area that will be the focus of treatment. Not only do the therapist and client do this together, but sometimes the therapist will temporarily hold off on the problem area that he or she may think is the most appropriate focus of treatment in favor of the one that the client prefers (Weissman et al., 2000). It is thought that if the client and therapist disagree about the appropriate treatment focus, allowing treatment to focus on the challenge of the client's choice may not only build a stronger therapeutic alliance but may also lead to a faster reduction of symptoms.

Collaborative work in IPT is also demonstrated by the therapist and client checking in with each other throughout the course of treatment. The therapist will ask for feedback on an experiment that the client has tried between visits, while the client may help the therapist to see why a certain communication style will not be effective, or may provide the therapist with some insight into the dissolution of a relationship that cannot be salvaged. In this way, the pair works together to provide the best treatment for the client, while still trying to fulfill the needs and desires of each party. Overall, IPT allows for the therapist and client to identify goals, to use strategies, and to adapt treatment to suit the individual needs of the client.

ROLE OF THE THERAPIST

In general, the IPT therapist is warm and supportive and tries to create a sense of optimism for the client, blaming the depression, as opposed to the client, when challenges arise. The therapist's position is generally optimistic, one of client advocate (Weissman et al., 2000, 2007) who supports the client particularly when feelings of helplessness and an attitude of pessimism may distress the client. While IPT therapists do not ignore clients' negative feelings in an effort to encourage optimism, the therapist's positive stance aims to offset the expected negativity expressed by the client that is often a function of his or her depression. The therapist provides genuine positive regard for the client, similar to that seen in Rogerian therapy but not to the same degree (Frank & Spanier, 1995). Although an IPT therapist demonstrates positive and supportive feelings toward the client, there is not an absolute acceptance of the client's behavior as in Rogerian therapy. Here, the therapist encourages the client to keep judgments of his or her interpersonal situation as realistic as possible (Frank & Spanier, 1995). In IPT, this means that the client's thoughts and feelings about interpersonal relationships, including the therapeutic relationship, are typically considered accurate assessments of the social situation (Weissman et al., 2000).

The IPT therapist cultivates a therapeutic atmosphere that reflects the goals of treatment. For example, the therapist is quite active in treatment sessions, working to maintain a focused treatment environment and structuring sessions so as to keep therapy on track. These characteristics of the therapist reflect the time-limited, focused nature of IPT. The therapist's position in many areas of IPT stands between extreme positions seen in some other psychotherapies. Pertaining to the active stance of the therapist, for example, Weissman and colleagues (2000) point out that the therapist may elicit material from the client to continue focused work on the treatment goals but that ultimately it is the responsibility of the client to make changes in treatment. Here we see how the therapist's stance is somewhere between "the extremes of being highly active and merely reactive to the patient's pro-ductions" (Weissman et al., 2000, p. 15). The therapist also plays an active role by brainstorming new interpersonal strategies, communication styles, and conflict resolution tactics with the client; providing psychoeducation about the client's depression when necessary; and role playing.

Moreover, negative transference is not explored in IPT, as might be done in psychoanalysis. When challenges arise in treatment, as evidenced by the client's arriving late to sessions, canceling sessions, or limiting participa-tion with the therapist, the therapist understands these symptoms to be sequelae of the depression, rather than negative transference to be addressed (Weissman et al., 2000). In part, because of the time-limited nature of IPT, often time does not allow for the exploration of underlying conflict held by the client. The therapist may use the time constraints of treatment to encourage the client's commitment to treatment and may remove self-criticism inflicted by the client by blaming the depression. Even outside of the time constraints of treatment, IPT does not explore intrapsychic defenses or internal conflicts as a way of explaining the client's depression; rather, depressive symptoms are discussed in relation to true interpersonal difficulties and the client's relationship to the outside world (Markowitz, Svartberg, & Swartz, 1998, as referenced in Markowitz & Swartz, 2007).

At times, however, using positive transference that develops in the therapeutic relationship may be advantageous to the client. Particularly for clients whose treatment focuses on interpersonal deficits, identifying the positive aspects of the therapeutic relationship and understanding how to apply these strategies to other social situations may arm the client with effective social skills. It is within the role of the therapist to point out these positive aspects of their relationship and to assist the client in implement-ing them in other relationships.

While IPT therapists do not regularly assign homework between ses-sions, the optimistic stance allows the therapist to encourage clients to try interpersonal "experiments" outside of sessions. The therapist then reviews the success or failure of an experiment and helps the client see what can be gained from the experience, praising the client for his or her attempts, regardless of the outcome. If the client does not succeed (or if he or she does not try the task at all), the fault is not placed on the client but is blamed on the depression. If failure occurs, the therapist will help the client set a goal that is more easily reached in an effort to improve morale. As well as asking the client to try out behavioral changes, the therapist will ask the client to use alternative ways of thinking and to consider new options to achieve interpersonal aims that previously were thought to be unfeasible. Overall, the therapist's stance may help to instill self-confidence in the client where this was previously wanting, as a result of the depression.

ROLE OF THE CLIENT

As is the case in a number of psychotherapeutic approaches, the client, like the therapist, is seen as having an active role in IPT. One of the first things the client is expected to do is to provide the therapist with honest and thorough information about his or her symptoms, expectations of treatment, and the information that makes up the interpersonal inventory. This implicit agreement about the client's interest and willingness to partake in therapy in an honest and open way is an underlying component of good work in therapy, as is the case in a variety of therapeutic techniques.

More specific to IPT, however, is that the client is expected to work collaboratively with the therapist in many areas of treatment. One example of this collaborative work is the client's agreement to a treatment contract that is set with the therapist. The client is not only expected to work on setting and agreeing to this contract but also to genuinely try to fulfill the guidelines of the contract. As noted above, this agreement generally includes information on the frequency of treatment, session duration, and other logistical considerations; however, it also includes an agreement on the problem area focus of treatment, confidentiality, and an understanding that work in treatment will focus on interpersonal and emotional content (Weissman et al., 2000). Within this contract, the client is expected to work toward the goals set out in the contract in these areas. Although it is typically not set out specifically within the treatment contract, the therapist and client often discuss the fact that the client is expected to contribute more and more to the session as treatment progresses (Weissman et al., 2000). Weissman and colleagues note that while the therapist is typically more vocal in the earlier stages of treatment, especially while gathering history and information for the interpersonal inventory, clients are expected to understand that "they will be responsible for choosing the topics in the remaining sessions and that the psychotherapist will be less active" (p. 56).

A few other expectations of the client play an integral part of successful work in IPT. One is the use of the sick role, which, if accepted by the client, may help the client to identify himself or herself as a person who is in an undesirable emotional state and in need of help. The hope is that temporary acceptance of this role will encourage collaborative work with the therapist toward getting well. Second, while homework is typically not assigned in IPT, at least in a formal sense, therapists will often ask the client to try out "interpersonal experiments" or to track the nature of an argument or communication with one's significant other (Stuart & Robertson, 2003). The client is expected to conduct this work outside of session with the understanding that it is often necessary to spend more than 1 hour per week on interpersonal problems in order to gain the maximum improvement possible, especially in a short-term treatment. Although similar in purpose to the homework often assigned in cognitive–behavioral therapy (CBT), the use of these experiments in IPT is much less structured than homework used in CBT and is typically not written. Outside work is not assigned at every session, but as the client and therapist deem appropriate based on the progress in treatment. This difference is likely based on the fact that the creators of IPT had worked in medical settings, where the structured homework used by behavioral psychologists was much less common, especially at that time.

Finally, although these are not requirements of treatment, it is beneficial for the client to enter therapy with an open mind about the potential use of medication, with a focused attitude toward interpersonal problems, and with the ability to explore and express emotions. It is hoped that the client will be open to the use of medication in addition to IPT if clinically indicated, as it has been shown that IPT and medication treatment work well together, at least for a subset of clients (c.f., Hollon et al., 2005). Not only does the medical model used in IPT allow for the successful addition of pharmacotherapy, but some clients are simply too depressed to conduct good work in therapy without the help of an antidepressant (Weissman et al., 2000). Second, as IPT is a short-term psychotherapy, it is not possible to cover all topics of an interpersonal nature during treatment. Thus, the client is encouraged to focus on the interpersonal problem that is most closely linked to the current depressive episode in an effort to resolve the depression as quickly and successfully as possible. As explained previously, this is not always possible if the client and therapist disagree about the primary focus of treatment. Still, the client is reminded of the time-limited nature of treatment and the importance of a focused strategy. Finally, and perhaps most important, it is essential for the client to be able and willing to explore and express emotions. Therapists in IPT often ask, "What are the feelings associated with that?" or "How did you feel when that happened?" The client's ability to engage in discussions of this nature is likely to facilitate improvement in interpersonal problems and reduction of depressive symptoms (Weissman et al., 2000).

BRIEF AND LONG-TERM STRATEGIES/ TECHNIQUES

Virtually all IPT sessions, regardless of which problem area is the focus, rely on several strategies that guide the sessions. These strategies may be used once or twice or may be more long-term techniques that are used repeatedly over the course of therapy. The purpose of these strategies is to aid the therapist in understanding the client's feelings and experience, to allow the client to see the effectiveness of the current techniques that he or she is using, to provide the client with an opportunity to truly experience his or her feelings and to understand their meaning, and to teach the client improved ways of communicating and interacting with others. These techniques may be used separately or in conjunction with one another, when appropriate, at the discretion of the therapist.

Despite the fact that several IPT strategies hone in on the interpersonal focus of treatment specifically, several techniques used by IPT therapists are common to many psychotherapies, and these are typically present in each therapy session to provide a rich therapeutic environment. Some of these more general techniques include the therapist's use of empathy to build a strong alliance and the use of open-ended questions to gather information from the client. Although other techniques may be considered long-term strategies of treatment, depending on the client's needs, empathy and open-ended questions are strategies that are used throughout the treatment and with all clients.

Setting the Tone of the Session

One strategy that sets the tone of each session is the opening question. The sessions usually begin with the therapist asking the client, "How have you been since we last met?" or "How has the last week been?" The purpose of this question is to remind the client of the present-focused nature of treatment (as opposed to a focus on the distant past), allowing the therapist to gather information about the past week. The client typically responds by reporting his or her current symptoms or recalling an event that happened since the last session. For example, the client may state, "My crying has let up a little bit, but I still have trouble falling asleep" for a symptom update, or "I didn't get the promotion I was hoping for" as a description of a recent occurrence related to the problem area on which the treatment has been focused. Regardless of where the client begins, the therapist finds a way to link the client's current distress or improvement to the events that have transpired since the last session. This continues to serve as a reminder to the client that his or her depression exists in a social context. At the beginning of therapy, the therapist emphasizes this connection purposefully, in order for the client to truly understand its importance and to learn to make the connection independently. As the client gains an understanding of the importance of this connection and grasps the general format and focus of treatment, the therapist may link interpersonal events and mood less overtly. Nonetheless, current symptoms and interpersonal events are addressed weekly.

The opening question is also an example of the type of open-ended questions that are used in IPT to encourage the client to expand on what is being discussed. Here, open-ended questions promote the client's exploration of the topic at hand, both for the therapist to gain information about the client and for the client to process the current topic more fully (Weissman et al., 2007).

Eliciting Details

Another ongoing strategy of the IPT therapist is to elicit a large amount of detail from the client when any type of interpersonal experience is described. Understanding a conversation, event, or the client's reaction to a social interaction at such a specific level of detail can assist the therapist in assessing the client's communication patterns, comprehending how conflicts originate, and identifying the ways in which these interactions affect the client's mood. Clients are asked to elaborate on specific details of the interpersonal experiences for two purposes: first, elaboration increases the therapist's effectiveness in identifying where the client may have gone awry and then in modeling for the client how to have healthier relationships; second, reviewing the experience, and the feelings associated with it, in such detail can be an important curative process for the client. Thus, delving into specific detail allows the client a second (and perhaps different) look at an interpersonal experience while providing the therapist with important details about the client's interactions. Most important, this specific recollection of events and feelings allows the therapist, once again, to make the connection between interpersonal events and depressive symptoms for the client.

Encouraging Expression of Affect

The expression of affect is encouraged by a number of different therapeutic orientations and is strongly and repeatedly emphasized in IPT. The encouragement of affect expression primarily allows the client to identify his or her true and often hidden feelings about a situation or person and generally supports the client's exploration of himself or herself as a person with emotions. This strategy may also assist the client in making a decision or implementing changes based on the emotions that are identified (Weissman et al., 2007). While this strategy is similar to elicitation of detail in that it increases the therapist's awareness of the client's experience, it differs in that expressing emotions is typically thought to be more cathartic than recalling specific details. Exploration of affect is not only necessary for the client to manage emotions more effectively, but Weissman and colleagues (2000) explain that "dealing with affect is essential in bringing about changes" (p. 126). Moreover, they explain that encouragement of affect facilitates the acceptance of unchangeable painful emotions, informs the client of how an interpersonal situation might change, and allows the client the opportunity to acknowledge previously unknown emotions. Encouragement of affect is one of the most widely used long-term strategies available to IPT therapists.

Communication Analysis

Poor communication often contributes to a client's relationship difficulties. Communication analysis, a short-term technique used particularly when addressing role disputes, assists the client in identifying where his or her communication may have gone awry in order to improve communication for the future. While this technique is used quite often with individuals whose difficulties focus on the role disputes problem area, it can be used effectively with clients in all problem areas. The therapist elicits from the client a conversation he or she has had with the other party to the dispute or with another significant individual. The therapist and client work through the details of the conversation, with the client recounting exactly what was said (Klerman et al., 1984). The therapist listens for communication patterns that may contribute to the client's difficulty, including ambiguous and indirect verbal and nonverbal communication, incorrect assumptions, or silence. The pair then works together to brainstorm ways that the client might have expressed his or her sentiments more effectively. Klerman and colleagues (1984) remind us that although poor communication can make an argument worse, it can also create difficulties between individuals where conflict did not previously exist. Thus, communication analysis can be vital for a client to clearly express the sentiments he or she may be feeling without running into interpersonal difficulty.

Use of the Therapeutic Relationship

As discussed previously, IPT does not encourage addressing transference in the therapeutic relationship, but examining the relationship may give the therapist an idea of the typical ways in which the client interacts with others. For example, understanding how the client feels about the therapeutic relationship may provide some insight into assumptions and attitudes that the client brings to most interpersonal relationships.

Likewise, the therapist's acknowledgment and examination of feelings that he or she may have about the client during their interactions can serve as a way to identify and understand similar feelings that other individuals in the client's life may also have. For example, a client whose therapy focuses on role disputes may be having consistent arguments with his wife. In session, the therapist notices that the client often cuts him off in the middle of a sentence and does not often respond directly to a question the therapist has asked. At times, this brings up irritation or even anger in the therapist; the therapist may guess that the client's wife feels similarly if the client's communication style with his wife is similar to that of therapy sessions. This may suggest that the client's communication style may be contributing to some of the intense arguments with his wife. This technique is also especially useful when working with individuals whose problems focus on interpersonal deficits; the therapist may use the therapeutic relationship to model for the client what a more healthy relationship might look like.

Psychoeducation

Psychoeducation is quite often implemented in IPT, particularly for a client whose episode of depression is his or her first. Even when working with clients who have experienced depression previously, the therapist can use psychoeducation to normalize the client's experience and to continue connecting the onset of the depression with the client's interpersonal difficulties. The client is reminded that the challenges he or she currently faces are the result of an illness, not the fault of the client, and that with some effort on the client's part, treatment is likely to be successful (Weissman et al., 2000). The therapist can also use psychoeducation to teach the client about how to have more positive interactions with others. This is particularly true when working with individuals whose difficulties focus on the interpersonal deficits problem area and who simply may not have the skills necessary to make these improvements.

Behavioral Activation

Although behavioral activation might be considered a cognitive–behavioral technique, when linked to the specific problem area focus, it also has a clear role in IPT. Thus, in role transitions work, a client might be encouraged to become newly engaged or reengaged in tasks and activities, such as attending a reading at the local library or taking a walk with a friend, as a way of renewing connections with others or creating new ones. Although adjunctive pharmacotherapy may help with this challenge, behavioral activation may also be effective in lifting the client's mood, which may allow for more productive therapy sessions. Other active strategies commonly used in IPT include decision analysis, or exploring options, and role playing.

Decision Analysis

Decision analysis, or exploring options, is a technique used frequently in IPT that helps clients identify alternatives within a situation in which they feel immobilized. Once these alternatives are identified, the therapist teaches the client to consider and weigh these options when making a decision as to how to proceed (Weissman et al., 2007). Depressed clients may not always see all options available to them because of their current mood and cognitive state. In turn, this feeling of immobility can lead depressed clients to assess situations as being more hopeless and having fewer options than may truly be the case. The therapist supports the client in weighing the advantages and disadvantages of the viable options that the client identifies and helps the client come up with new alternatives that may not have been identified previously. Sometimes, the therapist can suggest helpful options that the client may have overlooked (Klerman et al., 1984). Exploring options may also include envisioning the realistic consequences of a new option that may have been previously unseen. However, the overarching goal of this technique is for the client to independently generate possible options when dealing with a situation and to choose one that is likely to provide a good outcome with regard to both mood and interpersonal relationships. Although the therapist does not guide the client to make one decision over another, he or she facilitates the process through which the client weighs the likely outcome of each alternative (Weissman et al., 2000).

Role Plays

Role plays are typically a short-term strategy that can be quite helpful in assisting a client to understand his or her feelings in a situation, to assess the effectiveness of his or her communication style, and to increase self-confidence (Weissman et al., 2007). Role plays also have the advantage of enabling the client to try out new ways of communicating with others within a controlled environment (Weissman et al., 2000; 2007). The therapist's office provides a safe place for the rehearsal and fine tuning of the skills that may improve the client's communication style. As Weissman and colleagues (2000) point out, role playing can be a critical step between a theoretical discussion of how the client would like to change his or her interpersonal style and the actual implementation of these changes in social settings. Role plays can also be used in conjunction with communication analysis; once a new way of communicating has been identified and agreed upon, the therapist and client may rehearse how the communication strategy will be utilized in a hypothetical situation.

The Role of Culture

As when adapting IPT for other disorders, modifications may be necessary to take into account cultural considerations of various populations. These considerations include financial concerns, barriers to treatment, and the need to adapt IPT for diverse settings, languages, and cultural customs and to address the stigma of treatment that may be more pronounced in certain cultures. As will be seen in Chapters 5 and 6 on the evaluation and future development of this form of therapy, adaptations of IPT for various cultures have been generally successful. In these chapters, we discuss consideration of these concerns in the use of IPT in rural Uganda, in rural mental health settings in this country, for low-income clients, and in some of the most recent adaptations of IPT that are still in development.

AN EXAMPLE OF AN IPT MODIFICATION: MAINTENANCE IPT

This section is provided to demonstrate how IPT in its original form may be modified and how this modified version may be implemented. Here, we focus on maintenance IPT (IPT-M), which is used once the client has responded to treatment of the acute depressive episode. This section is intended to describe how the primary process mechanisms and format of IPT may be adapted for a different treatment purpose.

IPT-M maintains the key characteristics of IPT, but the treatment goals, the number of problem areas addressed, the timing, and the focus of treatment are modified somewhat (Frank, 1991). The overall goal of IPT-M is to prevent recurrences of depression. A client entering the maintenance phase of treatment should have already reached remission, so the focus of IPT-M is on maintaining the well state. The client and therapist work collaboratively to watch for signals of a return of depressive symptoms that may have preceded the onset of previous depressive episodes as well as for interpersonal disturbances or challenges that might trigger a depressive episode (Frank, 1991). The client and therapist then work together to prevent the return of depression.

The four problem areas of IPT are maintained in IPT-M, although a greater number of problem areas is typically addressed over the course of IPT-M, which may last for several years (Frank, 1991). Based on the longer course of treatment and the fact that long-standing interpersonal patterns may become the focus of therapeutic work, it is common that at least two of the IPT problem areas will become the focus of treatment. One major role transition that is almost always explored in IPT-M is that of depressed person to well person (Frank, 1991). Clients being treated with IPT-M may have been depressed for enough of their lives that the new role as a well person, while welcomed, may be unfamiliar and somewhat frightening. The therapist guides the client to examine the positive and negative aspects of his or her situation, as would be done with other role transitions. A focus on the grief problem area is rarely the case in IPT-M unless a death actually occurs during treatment (Frank, 1991). Still, if a grief reaction arises during treatment, the strategies used to resolve grief in acute IPT (Klerman et al., 1984) may be utilized.

The timing of IPT-M also differs from that of acute IPT (Frank, 1991). Since the goal of treatment is now to prevent depressive recurrences, sessions are scheduled less often over a longer period of time, typically occurring once per month for several years. Clients in IPT-M are less symptomatic and require less frequent contact. But given the aim of resolving some of the more chronic interpersonal and personality difficulties faced by the clients, consistent and enduring treatment seems to suit these clients quite well.

While some clients may have no difficulty when transitioning from weekly to monthly sessions, some may experience this change as a loss (Frank, 1991). In this case it is recommended that the therapist address the client's discomfort in order to resolve his or her feelings of discouragement or anger at the loss of more frequent contact. On the other hand, based on the experience of the Maintenance Therapies in Recurrent Depression study (Frank et al., 1990), transitioning to monthly sessions may actually be beneficial for some clients, especially those who benefit from the use of the increased time between sessions to examine their concerns. In this case, monthly treatment may be more therapeutic than continuing with weekly sessions. Application of IPT-M in research settings will be described in Chapter 5.

OBSTACLES OR PROBLEMS USING THIS APPROACH

In this section we outline some of the obstacles that make the use of IPT less effective than desired. Nearly every therapeutic modality has some obstacles intrinsic to its methods that make its use more difficult, particularly with some client populations or when treating certain disorders. For IPT, those factors generally focus on a client's lack of focus or difficulty dealing with emotions, as well as individuals who are more somatically focused.

Characteristics of Depressed Clients

A major focus of treatment in IPT is on identifying and processing feelings. Individuals who have a hard time recognizing and working with their own feelings may have some difficulty in IPT. Clients who are particularly loquacious and/or tangential may also have a difficult time focusing on important themes in treatment or may be unable to work on an issue sufficiently before switching focus. In part because of the short-term nature of treatment, clients who lack the ability to focus may have a hard time making substantial progress in any one area. Likewise, clients who have concerns that supersede their depression or other psychiatric symptoms may have a hard time focusing on IPT strategies; these concerns might include substance dependence and legal problems or financial concerns.

Moreover, it may be challenging for clients whose psychopathology presents primarily somatically, such as those with comorbid anxiety, to focus on anything other than their somatic state. Behavioral changes suggested by the therapist may also increase the client's anxiety, making it harder to engage in adaptive changes.

Some of these challenges add to the difficulty that has been found in using IPT with individuals with alexithymia, substance abuse, and anxiety. Although adaptations to IPT are being developed and tested to address the specific needs of these client groups, individuals with these characteristics may have a more difficult time overcoming the obstacles listed above. We present a description of some of the obstacles faced when IPT is used to treat individuals with alexithymia in the next section. Following this section, we describe some trials of IPT for various disorders that have demonstrated reduced efficacy, perhaps because of some of the obstacles described above.

Individuals who suffer from symptoms of alexithymia in addition to their depression may be treated less successfully with IPT than clients who do not suffer from these symptoms (Lanza di Scalea, Cyranowski, Gilbert, Siracusano, & Frank, 2006). Alexithymia refers to an emotional disturbance in which the client experiences difficulty identifying, differentiating, and describing feelings, as well as difficulty differentiating between somatic sensations and emotions (Lanza di Scalea et al., 2006). Alexithymia is likely to be comorbid to other mood and anxiety disorders and symptoms (Honkalampi, Saarinen, Hintikka, Virtanen, & Viinamaki, 1999; Lumley, 2000). Given this, it may be particularly difficult to treat these clients with IPT, because such a large focus of treatment is on the awareness and expression of affect, precisely the skill that appears underdeveloped in this group.

In fact, a recent study demonstrated that clients with alexithymia may not fare as well in treatment, based on the fact that residual depressive symptoms that were present after treatment ended were predicted by alexithymic traits (Ogrodniczuk, Piper, & Joyce, 2004). Nonetheless, Lanza di Scalea and colleagues (2006) suggest the use of *some* IPT techniques as a way of beginning to decrease the client's depression. Practical tools such as exploring options, communication analysis, behavioral activation, psychoeducation, and role plays may improve the client's interpersonal relationships (thereby improving the depression) without getting into areas that are so challenging for alexithymic clients.

In a role dispute, for example, instead of focusing on the emotions that surround the conflict, it may be more successful to discuss what the client is seeking in the relationship and to identify ways in which he or she can modify current interpersonal skills to increase their efficacy. Communication analysis of problematic interpersonal interactions and role playing more successful future interactions may be effective practical tools for these clients. Those who suffer grief reactions but have difficulty identifying the emotions they have about the event may find some relief by focusing on behavioral activation techniques, in which the client can become more involved in new and renewed social activities. These tools may initiate the reduction of symptoms while clients slowly learn to access and identify emotions over the long term.

Challenges in Using IPT With Some Other Disorders

Several groups have had considerable success in modifying IPT for use with certain other disorders and populations, and these are discussed below; however, use of unmodified IPT to address some of the challenges described above have met with less success. For example, use of IPT for the treatment of anxiety disorders or as a treatment for depression in clients with comorbid anxiety has proven somewhat difficult. Not only is the presence of comorbid anxiety in depressed clients associated with a lower probability of remitting from depression (Feske, Frank, Kupfer, Shear, & Weaver, 1998), but clients who report the lifetime experience of panic-agoraphobic symptoms demonstrate a poorer response to treatment than those who do not report such symptoms (Frank, Shear, et al., 2000). As noted above, this is likely because the somatic symptoms that they report that may prevent them from focusing on interpersonal strategies and themes, or because of the anxiety that may arise when asked to engage in new behavioral experiments. However, in an open trial of treatment for panic-agoraphobic symptoms using a modified version of IPT, clients with this pathology showed some improvement in symptoms (Cyranowski et al., 2005), suggesting that an adaptation of IPT may be helpful for the treatment of anxiety disorders.

On the other hand, a recent trial of a modified version of IPT for the treatment of social anxiety disorder found that the therapy was not more helpful than supportive therapy, although the clients did show some improvement (Lipsitz et al., 2008). Likewise, in a trial comparing IPT and cognitive therapy in residential settings, residential IPT (RIPT) did not demonstrate a superior response to residential cognitive therapy (RCT) for the treatment of social phobia (Borge et al., 2008). Again, the anxiety surrounding engagement in social activities or new social roles may be an obstacle that is difficult for these individuals to overcome.

While IPT effectively treats depression, it has shown less success for the treatment of dysthymia. This may be a result of the difficulty of treating such a chronic illness with a relatively short-term therapy. Although dysthymic clients treated with a modified form of IPT did show some improvement, they did not improve as much as those who received sertraline or the combination of these treatments (Markowitz, Kocsis, Bleiberg, Christos, & Sacks, 2005; Steiner et al., 1998). A maintenance form of IPT may be more suitable. IPT has also demonstrated limited success for individuals who report substance abuse. Previous trials reported difficulty in recruiting this population, and those who were treated with IPT exhibited difficulty in abstaining from the abused substance (Carroll et al., 2004; Carroll, Rounsaville, & Gawin, 1991; Rounsaville, Gawin, & Kleber, 1985). As described above, clients with this challenge may have difficulty focusing on the interpersonal strategies employed by IPT while trying to overcome a focus on obtaining the abused substance or while withdrawing from the substance.

Case Examples Showing IPT in Action
Role Transitions

Ms. A is a 28-year-old Chinese-born graduate student who is currently finishing her PhD in statistics. She is the only child of Chinese parents who are both living. The client moved to this country 5 years ago to attend graduate school and remained in the United States for postdoctoral training. She has recently accepted a lucrative job in her field and has decided to stay in the United States for the long term. Six months ago, Ms. A became engaged to her boyfriend of 5 years, who she met at the start of graduate school. They are planning to marry in 6 months. In addition to recently being diagnosed with depression, Ms. A was also diagnosed with multiple sclerosis (MS) about 9 months ago. The client reports that she is in good health otherwise and that she had never experienced depression prior to this episode, although she does report noticing some depressive symptoms immediately after she arrived in this country for graduate school. However, Ms. A explains that these symptoms diminished once she adjusted to U.S. university life and made some new friends.

Ms. A is currently seeking treatment for depression. She believes the onset of this depressive episode occurred roughly 6 months ago and identifies the precipitants to this depression as being diagnosed with MS, becoming engaged to her fiancé, and, most recently, accepting a job in the United States. While Ms. A explains that she is very much looking forward to her upcoming marriage and beginning her new job, she feels overwhelmed by all of the changes she currently faces. Additionally, Ms. A and her parents, who live in China, disagree strongly about the best course of treatment for both her depression and her MS. Ms. A's parents encourage her to use Eastern treatments rather than those prescribed by her Western doctors and to live a more traditional lifestyle that would not include such a high-stress job and that would incorporate other changes to reduce her chances of experiencing exacerbations. The client notes that the disagreements between her and her parents over how to deal with her MS have led to difficulties in their relationship.

In addition to low mood and frequent crying spells, the client reports difficulty concentrating and making decisions, feelings of guilt that she may have brought this depression on herself based on all of the recent changes she has made in her life, loss of appetite, and subsequent loss of weight. She also reports poor sleep and overwhelming fatigue. Ms. A reports that these symptoms have been worsening since she received the MS diagnosis. Accordingly, the therapist suggested that a trial of antidepressant medication might be appropriate. Ms. A and her therapist discussed the advantages of adding pharmacotherapy, as well as any concerns that Ms. A had. The client agreed to meet with a psychiatrist for consultation.

Ms. A and her therapist conceptualized her treatment as focusing on role transitions. While she is facing a significant dispute with her parents, it appears that her depression is more the result of her recent diagnosis of MS and of the multiple role transitions she faces. In arriving at a decision as to which problem area to focus on in Ms. A's initial treatment, the therapist reviewed what had been discussed so far, including current symptoms and concerns, current interpersonal difficulties and recent life events. The therapist presented to Ms. A the idea that she is trying to adapt to a transition from girlfriend to wife, postdoctoral fellow to full-time employee, and well person to person with a chronic illness. After presenting these ideas, the therapist asked Ms. A for her reactions and asked whether Ms. A agreed that focusing on the challenges related to these transitions would be acceptable to her. Ms. A agreed that these were her most pressing concerns at present and that focusing treatment on transitions felt appropriate. She also agreed that the current conflicts with her parents were secondary to, and likely the result of, her attempts to deal with her new reality of having a chronic illness.

These transitions, especially occurring simultaneously, appeared to cause distress to Ms. A, as she is having some difficulty giving up her old roles even though she is looking forward to some of the new ones. It is easy to understand how a transition to a person with a chronic illness may cause distress, but even embracing the new roles that the client has sought out—wife and full-time employee—may trigger some depressive symptoms if the change in one's conception of oneself is sufficiently overwhelming. For example, Ms. A is somewhat nervous about moving in with her fiancé and how their relationship may change as a result of this lifelong commitment. Knowing how difficult it was for her to make the transition to American university life, she is also worried about how she will fit in with American corporate life. Treatment has focused on identifying the feelings associated with giving up each of those roles and taking on the new ones. The therapist encouraged Ms. A to realistically identify the positive and negative parts of the old roles and to hypothesize about what she can look forward to with the new ones. This process was difficult for Ms. A at first, because talking about the changes was somewhat frightening and made them feel more real to her. Eventually, Ms. A was able to acknowledge that while she will be giving up pieces of old roles that she liked, she will be giving up pieces that were not pleasing to her as well. This strategy facilitates the client's achievement of the major goal in the role transitions problem area, which is to identify the positive and negative aspects of the old and new roles in order to ease the current transition; the client was able to use this technique to avoid idealizing her old roles and to take a realistic view of them instead.

In Ms. A's case, the therapist made use of many of the classic IPT techniques, including giving the client the sick role, encouragement of affect, elicitation of detail, and identification of nonreciprocal role expectations. Ms. A was given the sick role primarily as a way of relieving some of the guilt and responsibility she felt as a result of performing relatively poorly in her postdoctoral work relative to her past level of achievement and not maintaining her social obligations. The therapist explained the concept of the sick role and the fact that this role might apply to her as a person with depression. In this case, Ms. A was also given the sick role in the context of being a person with a chronic illness. The therapist queried Ms. A in detail about how sick persons were treated in her native country and what expectations the society in which she grew up had of persons who were ill. Adapting her self-concept to identify herself as a person with depression and MS was a difficult process for Ms. A, but eventually helped her to mourn the "lost healthy self" and to accept herself in this new light.

In addition to enquiring in detail about how illness was handled in Ms. A's country of origin, her therapist used elicitation of detail to bring out the multiple ways in which Ms. A's role is currently changing: from single woman to wife, from visiting student to permanent U.S. resident, and from well person to a person with a chronic illness. Her therapist then used encouragement of affect to elicit her feelings about each of these transitions as a way of mourning the lost roles and embracing the new ones. This work was particularly challenging given cultural differences between the United States and China in terms of how and with whom one displays one's feelings. In order to help with this process, her therapist at first distanced the expression of affect work a bit by asking Ms. A to describe what she thought one of her American friends would say she was feeling in each of these situations. Being extremely clever, Ms. A soon caught on to this "ruse" and was able to say that she thought this technique would actually be helpful to her in her transition to U.S. resident.

As Ms. A's treatment did focus, in part, on the conflicts between her and her parents, her therapist also helped Ms. A identify the non-reciprocal role expectations between the parties. Ms. A reported that she expects her parents to accept her choice to live a more Western life-style, even though she feels it is likely that her parents would desire that Ms. A move back to China and try some Eastern treatments for her multiple sclerosis. Although Ms. A's parents were not able to come in for a session of treatment, the therapist and Ms. A were able to identify some ways in which she may be able to communicate her needs and expectations to her parents or to adjust these needs so as not to be in continued conflict with her parents.

Ms. A explained that while she is very excited about her new job, she is unsure of how much responsibility it will entail. She noted that she believes her symptoms are more the result of the uncertainty that surrounds the new job rather than the actual content of what she will be doing. Likewise, Ms. A is very much looking forward to her upcoming marriage, but she reports feeling overwhelmed with all that she has to do to prepare for the wedding. Moreover, she notes that this marriage likely means that she will be living in the United States for the majority of her life. While she does not have a desire to return to China, Ms. A reports sadness associated with the idea of living far away from her parents permanently and not being available to fulfill the responsibilities of a daughter as her parents age. Ms. A notes that she believes some of the arguments with her parents are truly the result of their feelings of sadness over this issue that manifest as disagreements over her treatment choices. In this way, Ms. A's status as a Chinese daughter was incorporated into treatment, primarily in an effort to understand the transition that she faces as she becomes a permanent American resident. The client and therapist discussed the aspects of Chinese culture that Ms. A will be giving up, as well as ways that she can incorporate her family's traditions into her new culture. In some way this was another transition for the client and required that she identify the aspects of her background that she will miss, but also identify the new traditions and cultural associations that she will gain through life in the United States.

After about 4 months of treatment, Ms. A still reports stress associated with wedding-related responsibilities, but her depressive symptoms have reduced significantly. She attributes this change to getting a better understanding of her emotions regarding all of these life changes. The client explains that she continues to modify her attitudes toward her new roles each day, but that she feels better equipped to handle these changes now that she understands the feelings that surround them. Additionally, Ms. A explains that by mourning the loss of her old roles, she has been much more able to let them go and to embrace the new roles that are on the horizon.

Role Disputes

Mr. C is a 20-year-old Caucasian male who is seeking treatment for depression. The client is in his second year at a community college and is the first person in his family to attend college. He is studying to be a radiology technician and has been living at home in an effort to save money. As his parents divorced during his high school years, he splits his time between his father's and his mother's houses, but he spends most nights at his father's house as he is able to provide a more spacious living environment for Mr. C. The client has one older brother who lives approximately 600 miles away. He reports that he and his brother speak on the phone every few weeks and that his brother comes home a few times per year. The client explains that he is fond of his brother, but since he does not have the opportunity to see him very much, his brother is not a significant figure in his life. Mr. C reports that he gets along well with his mother most of the time, but that his relationship with his father is more difficult.

Mr. C had been doing well in school until about 3 months ago; this was roughly the same time as the onset of his depression. The depressive symptoms Mr. C reports include fatigue, difficulty falling asleep but oversleeping in the morning, awakening once or twice throughout the night with difficulty falling back to sleep, low mood, anhedonia, increased appetite, and difficulty concentrating on his studies.

His relationship with his father was always a bit rocky, but at this time Mr. C and his father also began getting into serious arguments. Mr. C identifies the underlying theme of their arguments as conflict over his father's involvement in his life. The client sees him as an authoritarian man who tries to exert too much control over him, a young man who is now in college. Unlike his mother, who Mr. C notes is more laid back about her expectations of her son, the client's father would like to be apprised of his academic successes and failures, his financial expenditures, and the individuals and organizations with whom he involves himself. Complicating the picture is the fact that Mr. C's parents have chronically disagreed about how much control to exert over their son's life. Now that his parents are divorced, Mr. C experiences two very different lifestyles, depending on with which parent he is spending time. His parents agreed that they would each set their own rules for their son at their respective houses since they cannot, and historically have not, agreed on limits for him. Moreover, Mr. C and his mother feel that the fact that the client is in college has necessitated the modification of some of these limits in recent years, a change that has been more difficult for his father to accept or enact.

Based on the recent conflict with his father, the therapist and Mr. C conceptualized the client's treatment as focusing on a role dispute. They agreed that the client's dispute with his father is in the renegotiation stage, as their fights, although intense, are really attempts to work out their differences. Mr. C's role dispute appears to cause him significant distress because of the ongoing tension that is present in his relationship with his father, his sadness about spending so much of their time together fighting, and the guilt he feels over not living up to his father's expectations of their relationship. Mr. C reports that he is not interested in moving out of his father's house; he simply wants to resolve their disagreements. He would also like his father to be a bit less intrusive and demanding. The therapist and Mr. C discussed in detail the issues that usually come up in the arguments he has with his father. He explained that conflict typically arises over his father's desire to be intimately involved in many aspects of his life, or to at least have knowledge of the activities and individuals with whom he is involved. In addition, Mr. C would like to make decisions regarding the courses he will take in his last years of school and his plans for after graduation without his father's input, while his father would like to know of his general plans and have a say in the outcome.

The therapist identified these problems as nonreciprocal role expectations and helped Mr. C to see that they are at the heart of his disputes with his father. This conceptualization fits nicely with our theoretical understanding of the role disputes problem area, as described above: These disputes are based on expectations held by each party to the dispute that are not shared by the other party. By embracing this concept, Mr. C was able to explore the ways in which both he and his father may have unreasonable expectations of the other based on each wanting more control than the other is willing to give. As the client felt it might be possible for him and his father to resolve some of their differences, Mr. C's father was invited to attend a session with Mr. C and the therapist. This meeting allowed Mr. C's father and the client to understand how the other was feeling with regard to this dispute and to brainstorm some ways in which they could each alter their expectations to provide a healthier and more positive relationship. In sessions in which his father was not present, Mr. C and the therapist also used communication analysis to understand the ways in which his communication style was not working as effectively for him as it could. They practiced new ways of communicating together for later use with Mr. C's father. While the client's relationship with his father did not change dramatically over the course of treatment, Mr. C and his father have been able to communicate more openly, to understand the other person's point of view, and to make changes in their relationship where possible. Mr. C reported a decrease in his depressive symptoms with these positive changes.

Case Example With a Long-Term Client

Ms. E is a 42-year-old Afro-Caribbean woman who presented for treatment of her second episode of depression with IPT. She has been married for 15 years and resides with her husband. Ms. E and her husband have a 14-year-old son who has mental retardation. He had resided with the family until about 5 months ago, at which time he entered a group home in a distant suburb of their home city. Ms. E's mother lives in Jamaica; however, Ms. E does not see her very often. Her father had also resided in Jamaica until he passed away from an unexpected heart attack about 2½ years before the start of treatment. Ms. E's father had visited the client in the United States just a few months before his death. Ms. E also has a sister who is 3 years younger than she. Her sister is married and lives in a neighboring town, about 10 to 15 minutes away.

Ms. E had separated from her husband about 7 or 8 months prior to the start of treatment because of marital conflicts related to disagreements over their plans for their son and because of cultural differences between them. During that time, Ms. E lived with her sister, brother-in-law, and their two children.

The client began feeling somewhat depressed after her father passed away. In response to her concerns, her primary care physician (PCP) prescribed an antidepressant. Although her symptoms improved for a time, Ms. E's husband was against the idea of her taking the medication, so she did not refill the prescription. Despite the conflicts between them and the limited support that had motivated Ms. E to move out, the couple reconciled 6 months after they separated, about 1 month prior to the start of treatment. As noted above, Ms. E's and her husband's conflicts primarily centered on disagreements related to their son's placement. Once they were able to come to a decision about this, the conflicts between them lessened and they reconciled. The client and her husband also experience some cultural differences that fuel some arguments. While Ms. E is Afro-Caribbean, her husband is African American and was born and raised in the United States. The arguments pertaining to their cultural differences were exacerbated by the stress they experienced while deciding about their son's future. Their current arguments do not even approach the level of intensity that they did prior to their son's placement.

As she described in the interpersonal inventory at the start of treatment, Ms. E grew up in Jamaica with her parents and sister. She described her childhood as "typical." She met developmental milestones on time, did well in grade school and high school, and reported a number of close friendships throughout her school years. Ms. E began working in restaurants and coffee shops after graduating from high school, but she and her sister decided to move to the United States when she was 22 years old to be able to earn money to send back to their parents. Ms. E's mother was a homemaker and taught Sunday school at their church. Her father was a taxicab driver. The family experienced financial strain, which Ms. E noticed from a very young age. Ms. E reported that she had a close relationship with her father, but that he worked long hours driving the taxi and she wished that he had been around more often when she was growing up. Ms. E and her mother have always gotten along well, but they were never emotionally close.

When she moved to this country, Ms. E began working independently as an aide and companion to elderly individuals. She helps them with errands, cleaning, and preparing meals. Although she enjoys this work, it is sometimes stressful and the work is not always easy. Ms. E does get emotional support from her sister, although the level of that support is not as great as she desires. Her sister has stresses of her own related to her children. The client is also very involved in her church, from which she garners a great deal of support. Once each season for the past 5 years, Ms. E had helped to organize a charity fundraiser for her church, although she has not been involved during the past winter or spring because of her depression and the family difficulties she has been facing.

During the initial phase of treatment, the therapist also inquired about Ms. E's history of previous episodes. Ms. E has had one prior episode of depression, which occurred roughly 15 years ago when she moved to this country from Jamaica. The episode lasted approximately 1 year. Ms. E did not seek formal psychological treatment at the time, both because of the cost and because it was not a common practice in her country of origin. Instead, Ms. E sought counseling from her church's pastor. Although she only met with him for only a handful of sessions, she reported that the support and sense of belonging to her church were quite helpful to her. Ms. E's current episode of depression began soon after her father's death, roughly 2½ years prior to the start of her IPT treatment. As noted above, she saw some improvement while taking an antidepressant for about 3 months but discontinued use after that point. Ms. E noted that the use of psychotropic medications, even more than acknowledging a mental health problem, is not embraced by her culture or community. Thus, it has been hard for her to seek formal treatment or to revisit the idea of taking medication. Though she had recently sought out a few sessions of pastoral counseling, Ms. E felt that her depression had progressed to the point of requiring formal treatment, an idea to which she had become more accustomed the longer she lived in the United States. So, somewhat reluctantly, she sought psychotherapy at the outpatient clinic of the local psychiatric hospital.

At the beginning of treatment, Ms. E reported feelings of sadness, anger, guilt and worthlessness, reduced appetite, weight loss of roughly 8 pounds in the 2 months prior to initiating treatment, difficulty falling asleep, fatigue, and difficulty concentrating on housework. Ms. E reported that it was taking her at least an hour to fall asleep most nights and that she was forcing herself to eat "because she knows she needs to" even though she was rarely hungry. The client also reported crying spells several days each week.

Following the history taking and interpersonal inventory, Ms. E and her IPT therapist identified the precipitants to her depression as the death of her father, her son's placement in a residential facility, and the conflicts in her relationship with her husband. Ms. E's therapist suggested that they conceptualize the focus of her treatment as a role transition—or really a series of role transitions—arising from the recent stressful events in her life. Although the death of her father appeared to be the earliest precipitant to her depression, her symptoms seemed to have worsened considerably in relation to the more recent significant life changes, including her son's placement and the separation from her husband. In addition to the sadness and guilt she felt as a result of her father's death, Ms. E was also experiencing strong feelings of ambivalence about placing her son in a facility and about her relationship with her husband.

Ms. E's son was having significant behavior problems in the months prior to his placement that were not tolerated at the part-time treatment facility he was attending. Given her son's age and growing size, Ms. E was also having difficulty restraining her son when his behavior problems occurred. Ms. E and her husband chose to place their son in a facility in the rural suburbs of their city because there he receives the attention he needs and his behavior problems could be managed more successfully. While the facility is a good fit for her son, it presents significant practical problems for Ms. E. Using public transportation to visit him requires multiple buses and a lengthy trip. The couple shares a single car, and Ms. E uses public transportation to get to work on most days. This means that she can rarely visit her son without difficulty unless her husband is also available to go along or is able to relinquish their car. She reported feeling sad about not being able to see her son more often but recognizes that unless she and her husband both maintain their jobs, they will not be able to afford to pay for their son's care.

At the end of the initial phase, Ms. E and her therapist set the treatment contract. Given the numerous serious stressors in her life, Ms. E and her therapist contracted for a longer-than-typical course of IPT treatment that would allow her therapist to incorporate elements of grief work into a larger focus on role transitions. In a shorter treatment arrangement, the therapist likely would have focused the work specifically on the issue or issues that were most closely tied temporally with the onset of the client's current depressive episode; in Ms. E's case, however, the depression had been ongoing for a number of years, with worsening related to the roughly contemporaneous marital separation and separation from her child. By projecting a somewhat longer course of treatment, the therapist would be able to address the more recent life events related to the worsening of her depression as well as spend some more time learning about Ms. E's relationship with her father to add a focus on grief. In the end, Ms. E's course of IPT treatment lasted about 10 months.

In addition to these specific, event-related foci, Ms. E's therapist noted the general difficulty Ms. E was having in accepting her depression and treatment for it. Thus, he spent a full session during the initial phase asking her about her beliefs about depression and other mental illnesses, both in her culture of origin in Jamaica and in her religious and social community here in the United States. This discussion made it very clear to her therapist that Ms. E saw her depression as something quite distinct from other forms of illness. Ms. E noted that mental health problems are not publicly acknowledged or discussed in her community, which was part of the reason why she resisted seeking treatment and also why her husband discouraged her from continuing to take the antidepressant that had been somewhat helpful to her. Ms. E's therapist, therefore, spent considerable time prior to entering the middle phase of treatment presenting the medical model of depression and, within that model, normalizing the symptoms that she reported. This enabled her therapist to assign her the sick role, which, within her culture, clearly allowed for the ministrations of caring others. As Ms. E has had difficulty in the past accepting the idea of psychological treatment, it was easier to embrace psychotherapy once her condition was conceptualized as a medical one and the therapist's work was conceptualized as yet another form of ministration from others. She noted that if she could think of her symptoms as a medical condition, she would feel much more comfortable accepting treatment, even if she was not yet ready to share her symptoms with some close friends who often offer her support. Ms. E noted that thinking of depression as a medical condition was a huge relief to her, as she could begin to accept the idea that she did not do something to bring on the symptoms she had been having.

As a result of this discussion of the medical model, Ms. E also reconsidered the idea of taking an antidepressant. The medication seemed to help her in the past, but she was not eager to refill her prescription when her husband dismissed the idea. In her local community, requiring help of this nature is often seen as a weakness and can incite gossip among her peers. After discussing the use of medication within the context of the medical model over several sessions, Ms. E agreed to see her PCP to obtain another prescription. As she grew more comfortable with the idea of depression as a medical condition, her concern for what her peers would think was replaced with her concern for her well-being. The fact that the client had some additional time to become comfortable with the idea of medication treatment was another benefit of a longer course of IPT, especially since she had initially been so resistant to medication.

For Ms. E, the initial phase lasted about 5 weeks. She and the therapist spent the first few sessions reviewing her symptoms and completing the interpersonal inventory. During the remaining sessions they discussed Ms. E's concerns about accepting a diagnosis of depression. They reviewed the medical model and the sick role, they developed a shared conceptualization of her IPT problem area, and they set a treatment contract.

Treatment then moved into the middle phase, which lasted about 7 months. During this phase, Ms. E reviewed the events leading up to her father's death and the guilt she felt for not having spent more time with him in the past 15 years since moving to the United States. The client explained the mixed emotions she felt about having moved away from her parents, both the guilt she felt for not spending more time with them and the pride she felt in being able to send some money to them every month. Ms. E had not experienced these conflicting emotions in recent years, but the death of her father sparked a resurgence of these feelings. Ms. E and the therapist discussed the many positive aspects of her relationship with her father, but also addressed the few ways in which he had disappointed her both as a child and as an adult. Explaining to the therapist both the positive *and* negative parts of her relationship with her father prevented Ms. E from idealizing him or their relationship. Ms. E described her father's last visit to the United States in great detail, allowing her therapist to point out on what a good note Ms. E and her father had separated when they last saw one another. In particular, her father's recent visit pointed out to the client how much she missed spending time with him, and so she was especially upset by his death soon after. She reviewed her trip home for his funeral and processed the emotions she experienced during that time. In doing so, she was able to acknowledge how happy she was to have been able to be a part of his passing, how much respect other members of her family's community had shown him during the funeral, and how much that had meant to her.

Although grief work in IPT can often include finding other social supports who can take the place of the deceased, as Ms. E did not see or speak to her father very often, this was less of a concern. Still, Ms. E reported feeling like she was no longer a child since her father had passed, and she thought that she might turn to elder members of her church for advice in the future. This idea was particularly comforting to her.

During the middle phase, Ms. E and her therapist also focused a few months of their work on the recent stressful events in her life. They reviewed in considerable detail the multiple difficulties that Ms. E and her husband have faced in raising a disabled child, as well as all the things that brought them to the decision to send him to live in a group home. Ms. E feels tremendous guilt for sending her son to the suburban facility, even though she knows it will ultimately provide a better environment for him than she can provide at home or than might be offered in a facility closer to her home. In many ways, Ms. E feels as though she has lost her only child and is terribly saddened by this. Her therapist suggested that she view this role transition as similar to when one's child goes away to college or moves away from home for employment. They talked about the emotional and practical benefits of having her son live with her and her husband, but they also discussed the ways in which her son's presence in their home added a daily burden of stresses and of guilt feelings related to her needing to leave him with sitters to go to her job, the insufficient part-time care that he was receiving at their local treatment facility, and her inability to give him the kind of special education and training he would need to survive once she and her husband were no longer alive. They discussed what Ms. E will miss now that her son is not living with her, but they also discussed the benefits that her son may gain by being in an environment in which he is constantly attended by mental retardation specialists. As is the cornerstone of IPT, at each point in this discussion, the therapist asked Ms. E to describe the specific emotions she experienced in relation to the content of their discussion.

Ms. E also expressed concern that she would not have as much time as she would like to visit her son because of her busy work schedule and the difficulties in using public transportation to visit him. She may borrow her husband's car on occasion, but the majority of the time she is limited by the distance. While she and her husband can visit their son on some weekends, Ms. E still experiences guilt that this is not adequate. Ms. E and her therapist went through a systematic process of exploring options to map out Ms. E's priorities and to enumerate the ways in which she might be able to increase the frequency of her visits while also maintaining her income. Ms. E and the therapist spent two sessions on this work. As is typical in IPT, the therapist allowed the client to generate as many of the alternatives as she could, but he also added to that list when Ms. E was unable to think of additional strategies. Among other things, the therapist suggested that Ms. E might write more letters to her son as a way of feeling more connected to him.

Ms. E also described feeling lonely. When she and her therapist explored this further, Ms. E noted that in addition to missing her son, she has not felt as motivated to participate in the church activities in which she had taken part in the past and that had provided much of her social contact. Initially she stated that the church work would be too exhausting for her, given the limited energy she had since becoming depressed. When she and her therapist explored this further, it became clear that her church involvement really decreased during her marital separation, largely because she was embarrassed to see the other members of her community since she had separated from her husband. The therapist talked with Ms. E about reconnecting with her church group now that she and her husband had reconciled, both as a means of behavioral activation and as a way of decreasing her sense of loneliness. Ms. E noted that she would look forward to rejoining her church activities if she could find the energy, but was concerned that the other members of her church might not welcome her back warmly after her absence. Ms. E and the therapist role-played some return-to-church activity scenarios, enabling Ms. E to practice communicating her happiness to see her friends and how she might respond to questions about her absence and about her recent separation.

Reconnecting with her friends at church and rejoining the church activities in which she is normally involved became an important focus in this case because of how important the church community is in Ms. E's culture. The therapist recognized the importance of this aspect of Ms. E's life not only from the client's report of her recent activities and the strength she previously gained from her pastoral counseling sessions, but also from Ms. E's descriptions of her mother's activities as a Sunday school teacher in Jamaica. This seems to have made an impression on Ms. E from a very early age. Through discussions in the middle phase of therapy, Ms. E was able to recognize that she feels she maintains some connection with her parents through her involvement with her church. As her church activities increased, her mood improved steadily.

Once her mood was somewhat better and she was feeling stronger, approximately 6 months into treatment, Ms. E's therapist suggested that they begin to talk about the conflicts she had experienced with her husband that had led to the marital separation and to focus on how things had been going since she and her husband were together again. In addition to the initial disagreement regarding their son's living arrangements, the marital conflicts also focused on cultural differences between the couple.

For Ms. E, being involved in the church community and attending weekly services was an important part of her life. Her husband did not come from a family in which the church was as important, and so he declined to attend with Ms. E, even though her church was attended by individuals from a variety of cultures and backgrounds. The client saw this as a lack of support on her husband's part. On further reflection, Ms. E conceded that her husband felt pressured by her continued insistence that he attend church with her and that maybe, while it was a source of support and enjoyment to her, he simply did not share those feelings.

Ms. E and her husband also differed with respect to how they liked to spend the holidays throughout the year. Ms. E preferred to integrate aspects of her Jamaican culture into holiday meals and celebrations. As such, she has spent many of the holidays with her sister and her sister's family because they participate in Jamaican traditions. However, Ms. E's husband chooses not to participate in these traditions. Again, this is a source of contention between the two. Finally, Ms. E mentioned that although seeking mental health treatment is not widespread in her Jamaican culture, talking with friends and family members about one's concerns is a common practice. However, Ms. E's husband came from a family in which talking about one's feelings was not encouraged, so he does not often inquire about how Ms. E is feeling. In the end, Ms. E was able to see the multiple ways in which she and her husband held nonreciprocal expectations about their roles in one another's lives.

Resolving these issues focused on Ms. E's expectations in the relationship and identifying the places where she was and was not willing to modify those expectations. Ms. E talked with her husband about the importance of her Jamaican traditions, and they agreed to split the holiday times more equally between his family and hers. However, Mr. E was not willing to attend church or church-related activities with his wife, and Ms. E was eventually able to view that as a reasonable choice on her husband's part rather than a rejection of her. Ms. E and the therapist identified other people with whom she could share these pursuits, such as her group of friends who also attend church with her. Once Ms. E became more comfortable with the idea of reengaging in social activities, she was happy with the idea of using these social contacts as support.

Coming to terms with the recent changes in her life, resolving some of the conflicts in her relationship with her husband, processing the grief she reported for her father, and accepting her depressive illness and the benefits of both psychotherapy and pharmacotherapy together led to a complete resolution of Ms. E's depression. During the final phase of treatment, roughly the last month, Ms. E and her therapist reviewed the work they had done together and the progress Ms. E had made. She had come to view her son's placement not as a loss or a demonstration of her lack of caring for him, but as a necessary and even courageous step in his long-term care. After a discussion of the medical model through which depression is viewed in IPT, the client was able to begin another trial of pharmacotherapy. Although open discussion of mental health problems and the use of pharmacotherapy are not embraced in her community, the therapist's use of the medical model and provision of the sick role eventually allowed Ms. E to feel comfortable using the resources that would benefit her most. As she began to feel better, Ms. E was able to reengage in some of the activities at her church in which she had previously participated, thus decreasing her social isolation and loneliness. She and the therapist prepared her to transition back to this part of her life with role plays. Finally, Ms. E worked to modify some of her expectation of her relationship with her husband. She was able to share with her husband that she would like to participate in some of her Jamaican holiday traditions with her family, but that she could participate in church activities without him. Instead, she would find support there from her friends who also attended church. Finally, treatment with IPT allowed Ms. E to process the feelings of guilt and sadness she experienced after the death of her father and come to terms with her own role as an adult.

5

Evaluation

This chapter reviews studies on the use of interpersonal psychotherapy (IPT) for depression and a number of adaptations to IPT that have been developed since its inception. It focuses on the efficacy of IPT, both as a treatment for acute depression and in a maintenance format. Then, the areas where this approach is and is not effective are discussed, as well as applications of IPT for individuals with other psychiatric and medical diagnoses. Finally, this chapter describes the use of IPT for diverse client populations worldwide.

Portions of this chapter have been reprinted and adapted from "Interpersonal Psychotherapy," by C. L. Cornes and E. Frank, 1996, in L. J. Dickstein, J. M. Oldham, and M. B. Riba (Eds.), *Review of Psychiatry*, 15, pp. 91–108. Copyright 1996 by American Psychiatric Association. Adapted with permission; and "Interpersonal Psychotherapy for Unipolar and Bipolar Disorders," by H. A. Swartz, J. C. Markowitz, and E. Frank, 2002, in S. Hoffmann and M. Tompson (Eds.), *Treating Chronic and Severe Mental Disorders: A Handbook of Empirically Supported Interventions* (pp. 131–158). Copyright 2002 by Guilford Press. Reprinted with permission.

RESEARCH SUPPORTING EFFICACY OF THE IPT APPROACH

This section describes the efficacy of IPT for depression. Included here is the research supporting the use of IPT for acute depression in mid-life adults, postpartum women, depressed adolescents, late-life adults, and depressed mothers whose children are seeking mental health treatment. It will also review data showing the efficacy of IPT when used as a maintenance treatment for recurrent depression and in a group setting. Some information on the effects of client characteristics on the outcome of IPT is also included.

Acute Depression

Research on IPT has shown it to be an efficacious treatment for acute depression as compared to other treatment options (c.f., Hollon et al., 2005). The initial development and testing of IPT was conducted by Klerman, Weissman, and collaborators, as described in the 1987 review by Klerman and Weissman. The first study of IPT investigated the effects of amitriptyline and IPT on the relapse rate of 150 women who had recently recovered from a depressive episode. The study compared amitriptyline, placebo, and a no pill group, crossed with high and low contact psychotherapy groups, in terms of their effect on relapse rates (Klerman et al., 1974). The psychotherapy used in the study was not referred to as IPT, but rather a "once-a-week interview focusing on interpersonal, transactional relations of the client" (Klerman et al., 1974, p. 190). After 8 months of treatment there was no difference between pharmacotherapy alone and pharmacotherapy plus psychotherapy in preventing relapse, but those receiving psychotherapy showed a significant improvement in social adjustment (Klerman et al., 1974; Weissman et al., 1974; each as described in Klerman & Weissman, 1987).

Encouraged by these initial findings to continue investigating the effects of this treatment, the research group then conducted a study examining the effects of IPT, a control psychotherapy, amitriptyline, and the combination of IPT and drug over 16 weeks for the treatment of acute depression (DiMascio et al., 1979, as cited in Klerman & Weissman, 1987).

Both IPT and amitriptyline alone were each more effective than control psychotherapy; however, the combination of therapies was superior to either monotherapy (Klerman & Weissman, 1987). Moreover, clients who received IPT, alone or in combination with medication, were functioning better socially than those who had received either of the other treatments alone (Weissman, Klerman, Prusoff, Sholomskas, & Padian, 1981). More recently, Blom and colleagues (2007) conducted a study of 193 depressed individuals comparing the efficacy of IPT, nefazodone, IPT plus nefazodone, and IPT plus placebo to support the superiority of combination treatment. Ratings of depressive symptoms demonstrated that combined IPT and pharmacotherapy were superior to pharmacotherapy alone, as in the earlier study, but not superior to psychotherapy alone.

Based on the initial success of IPT, it was included as one of the treatments in the NIMH Treatment of Depression Collaborative Research Program (TDCRP) study. The other treatments were imipramine plus clinical management (CM), cognitive–behavioral therapy (CBT), and placebo plus CM. Elkin and colleagues (1989) reported that IPT was as effective as the other three treatments at reducing clients' depressive symptoms but was more effective than placebo plus CM among clients with more severe levels of baseline depression.

This finding was also supported by a more recent study of 124 depressed inpatients who were treated with IPT plus medication or intensive CM plus medication for 5 weeks. IPT was modified to include 15 individual sessions and 8 group sessions, while those randomized to CM plus medication received 3 weekly sessions of CM (Schramm et al., 2007). Those receiving IPT showed a greater reduction of depressive symptoms at the end of the acute treatment period, as well as greater treatment gains at 3-month follow-up, although there were no differences at 1-year follow-up.

Previous work has also identified the best treatment strategies using IPT for depressed clients. As described above, the acute phase of maintenance therapy studies conducted by our group point to the superiority of a sequential treatment approach, first implementing IPT and then adding pharmacotherapy for those clients who do not remit with IPT alone, over combination treatment from the outset of treatment in the absolute rate of remission of depressed clients (Frank, Grochocinski, et al., 2000).

Not surprisingly, this treatment strategy was associated with a longer median time to remission than beginning with combination treatment, but the final outcomes were superior. Thus, sequential treatment seems to be less costly and more beneficial than monotherapy or combination treatment from the outset of treatment. Overall, these initial reports constitute the foundational evidence for IPT as an effective treatment for acute depression.

Postpartum Depression

Stuart and O'Hara (1995) created a modified form of IPT to treat postpartum depression. Although IPT for this population resembles IPT as originally developed by Klerman and Weissman's group (1984), there is an added focus on the interpersonal changes that women experience during the postpartum period. Additionally, this form of IPT is typically 12 weeks, as opposed to the 16 to 20 sessions of IPT.

When used as a treatment for 120 postpartum depressed women, IPT more effectively reduced participants' depressive symptoms and improved their psychosocial functioning than a wait-list condition (O'Hara, Stuart, Gorman, & Wenzel, 2000). The authors note that IPT is well suited for postpartum depression as the very nature of the pathology revolves around a role transition. Most study participants experienced a series of changes in role—from pregnant woman to a woman with a child and from a wife, girlfriend, or single woman to mother.

The availability of IPT as an effective treatment for postpartum women with depression is especially important as postpartum women may have concerns about exposing their infants to antidepressant medication through breastfeeding (Pearlstein et al., 2006). A study of 23 postpartum women with depression confirmed this notion, showing a trend for women who were breastfeeding to choose IPT over a medication alone or combination treatment ($p = 0.10$) (Pearlstein et al., 2006). However, women with at least one prior episode of depression were more likely to choose sertraline alone or in combination with IPT as a treatment for their depression. Thus, the availability of IPT as an effective treatment without the risk of medicating the infant appears to be quite useful for postpartum and breastfeeding mothers.

IPT for postpartum depression has also been used successfully in a group format (Klier, Muzik, Rosenblum, & Lenz, 2001). While the initial and final stages of treatment resemble IPT in its original form, the middle stage of treatment includes group processes of interacting with other group members, acknowledging conflict and identification of coping mechanisms, and developing intimacy. This psychotherapy has shown to be an effective treatment in an open pilot treatment trial of 17 postpartum women with depression (Klier et al., 2001). More recently, a research group in Australia showed that depressive symptom scores significantly decreased after treatment with IPT in a group of postpartum depressed women, although these gains were not as great as those seen in individual IPT (Reay, Fisher, Robertson, Adams, & Owen, 2006). The authors suggest future studies to further support the effectiveness of group IPT for postpartum depression. Overall, however, the use of IPT for women with postpartum depression has been deemed an accessible and effective treatment (Grigoriadis & Ravitz, 2007).

Recent work has also been conducted on the use of IPT for depression that occurs during pregnancy. A preliminary study of IPT for this population compared IPT to a parenting education program. Treatment with IPT followed the original manual (Klerman et al., 1984), but a fifth problem area, complicated pregnancy, was added (Spinelli & Endicott, 2003). The authors report that clients receiving IPT showed significant improvement in mood as compared to the parenting education group after 16 weeks of group therapy. The authors also suggest that IPT should be considered a first-line treatment for antepartum depression.

Maintenance IPT for Recurrent Depression

The implementation of IPT as a preventative maintenance treatment (IPT-M; Frank, 1991) is based on the original form of IPT, developed by Klerman, Weissman, and colleagues (Klerman et al., 1984). The first study investigating the effectiveness of IPT (Klerman et al., 1974) used a preliminary form of IPT as a maintenance treatment for outpatients who had responded to 6 weeks of treatment for an acute depressive episode. From this initial study came the development of IPT for use in acute contexts; further research on IPT as a maintenance treatment did not occur until almost 10 years later. The initial investigation of IPT as a long-term maintenance treatment was the Maintenance Therapies in Recurrent Depression protocol (MTRD; Frank et al., 1990), in which clients with recurrent depression received IPT in acute, continuation, and maintenance contexts. Remitted clients who entered maintenance therapy received monthly IPT for up to 3 years or until they experienced a recurrence of depression.

The efficacy of IPT-M in preventing recurrences of depression has been demonstrated in a number of trials. The MTRD study showed the acceptability and effective implementation of this adaptation of IPT. Although IPT-M was not as effective a prophylactic as active imipramine, among individuals who were receiving IPT-M but no active medication, monthly IPT-M sessions over a 3-year period served to significantly lengthen the time to recurrence of depression relative to monthly clinic visits with no psychotherapy.

Subsequently, Reynolds and colleagues (1999) compared the efficacy of monthly IPT-M with nortriptyline, placebo, and IPT-M and nortriptyline combined in a sample of 180 depressed older adults. IPT-M and nortriptyline individually provided longer times to recurrence than placebo, and the combination treatment provided superior treatment than either treatment alone. The success of IPT-M was also supported more recently in a study of mid-life women with recurrent depression, in which women were treated acutely with IPT alone unless IPT monotherapy was insufficient to bring about a remission (Frank et al., 2007). Monthly IPT-M was shown to be as efficacious in preventing the return of depression as weekly or biweekly sessions. However, IPT-M was less effective as a maintenance treatment for women who required added pharmacotherapy to achieve remission. Overall, IPT-M appears to be a reasonable treatment option for clients with recurrent depression who seek to maintain their remitted status or lengthen time between episodes; however, in clients who required pharmacotherapy to achieve remission, IPT-M is probably best used in combination with pharmacotherapy.

IPT in a Group Setting

IPT has also been modified for use in a group setting (IPT-G). This treatment format not only has the possibility of reduced cost for clients but may also provide the opportunity for clients to improve interpersonal skills and receive increased social support (Weissman et al., 2000). Based on a model created by Wilfley and colleagues (1993), IPT-G still focuses on social roles and interpersonal relationships, but the group format provides an "interpersonal laboratory" in which to work on this focus. In the case of the group format, Weissman and colleagues (2000) note that interpersonal inventories are completed for each group member in an individual interview prior to beginning weekly 90-minute group sessions. IPT-G also has the advantage of reducing social isolation by providing a place for clients to discuss interpersonal problems, as well as to validate the sick role by sharing their illness with others (Weissman et al., 2007). For a more detailed description of IPT for group settings, see Wilfley and colleagues (2000).

Wilfley's group demonstrated the efficacy of IPT-G as a treatment for bulimia and binge eating disorder (Wilfley et al., 1993, 2002), which will be described in more detail in the section on eating disorders. IPT-G has also been used for clients with depression. In 2001, MacKenzie and Grabovac presented a study of 14-week IPT-G for this population, showing that while there was no treatment control group, five of the eight participants demonstrated significant reduction of depressive symptoms over the course of the treatment and at a 4-month follow-up. Further modifications of the use of IPT-G have included the treatment of postpartum women (Klier et al., 2001; Reay et al., 2006) and the treatment of PTSD (Robertson, Rushton, Batrim, Moore, & Morris, 2007). Although preliminary, this work suggests that modifications of IPT-G may be effective treatments for these disorders.

Mufson's group has also adapted IPT for adolescents (IPT-A) for use in a group setting (IPT-AG; Mufson, Gallagher, Dorta, & Young, 2004). This form of IPT allows clients to test newly acquired interpersonal skills and to receive feedback from peers. As will be described next, clients receiving IPT-AG have reported as much improvement in symptoms as clients receiving IPT-A, if not more (Mufson, Gallagher, et al., 2004).

IPT as a Treatment for Depressed Adolescents

The use of IPT to treat depressed adolescents (IPT-A) has received strong support (e.g., David-Ferdon & Kaslow, 2008). Developed by a group at Columbia University (Mufson, Moreau, Weissman, & Klerman, 1993),

IPT-A differs somewhat from IPT in its original form. IPT-A has a fifth problem area that focuses on problems associated with single-parent families and in the involvement of parents in the beginning of treatment. As well, IPT-A therapists often initiate contact with the adolescent client's parents and school later on in treatment and may contact the client via telephone between sessions. Family members may participate at times during therapy to improve communication within the family, to discuss progress, and to plan for management of interpersonal family issues that may arise after treatment ends (Brunstein-Klomek & Mufson, 2006).

IPT-A is typically shorter than IPT (12 weeks), and the sick role has a much more limited application. While the adolescent and his or her parents receive psychoeducation about depression, the client receives more encouragement to participate in everyday activities than is typically seen in IPT (Brunstein-Klomek, Zalsman, & Mufson, 2007). As the authors explain, this limited sick role motivates the adolescent to remain engaged in social activities and to be accountable for his or her actions.

After preliminary studies demonstrated the efficacy of IPT-A in a small sample (Mufson & Fairbanks, 1996; Mufson et al., 1994), Mufson, Weissman, Moreau, and Garfinkel (1999) studied the effectiveness of IPT-A in a group of 48 depressed inner-city adolescents who were mostly Latino. These adolescents received either 12 weeks of treatment with IPT-A or a clinical monitoring condition. Clients receiving IPT-A reported significantly greater improvement in social functioning and a greater likelihood of remitting (75% vs. 46%) than those in the clinical monitoring condition (Mufson et al., 1999). In a later project, Rosselló and Bernal (1999) demonstrated the superiority of IPT at reducing depressive symptoms over a wait-list condition in 71 depressed Puerto Rican adolescents. Clients who received IPT also reported significantly better self-esteem and overall functioning than clients who received CBT in this study (Mufson et al., 1999). A more recent study of IPT-A conducted in school-based mental health clinics again demonstrated the superiority of the treatment at improving overall functioning and reducing depressive symptoms relative to a control condition (Mufson, Dorta, Wickramaratne, et al., 2004).

As noted above, Mufson's group has also adapted IPT-A for use in a group setting (IPT-AG; Mufson, Gallagher, et al., 2004). Initial work on IPT-AG has shown more than the feasibility of the treatment: When compared to IPT-A, individuals receiving IPT-AG demonstrated as much improvement in symptoms as the individual treatment condition, if not more (Mufson, Gallagher, et al., 2004). IPT-AG includes 12 group sessions that are typically 90 minutes in length, and a few individual sessions that occur before, in the middle of, and after the last group session (Brunstein-Klomek & Mufson, 2006). IPT-AG may provide an opportunity for individuals to receive effective IPT treatment in a format that may be a more financially feasible treatment option.

Most recently, IPT-A has been adapted for use with pregnant adolescents (IPT-PA; Miller et al., 2008). Through two pilot studies, the authors showed that group IPT-PA is acceptable to this population and is associated with a reduction in depressive symptoms (Miller et al., 2008). In sum, IPT for depressed adolescents appears to be effective in a variety of treatment settings.

IPT for Late-Life Depression

IPT has been successfully used for the treatment of depression in late life. Early pilot studies showed a positive outcome for late-life depressed clients treated with IPT in an outpatient setting (Rothblum, Sholomskas, Berry, & Prusoff, 1982; Sholomskas, Chevron, Prusoff, & Berry, 1983). Sloane, Staples, and Schneider (1985) and Schneider, Sloane, Staples, and Bender (1986) also reported that older adults treated with IPT showed a positive outcome as compared to nortriptyline treatment. More recently, Miller et al. (1994) demonstrated the success of IPT for depressed bereaved spouses in late life.

Even more recently, the initial Maintenance Therapies in Late Life Depression (MTLD-I) study treated clients age 60 and older with recurrent depression using IPT. These clients were first treated in the acute phase with nortriptyline (NT) plus IPT-M and then randomly assigned to NT plus IPT-M, placebo plus IPT-M, NT plus clinical management (CM), or placebo plus CM for 2 years of maintenance treatment (Reynolds et al., 1999). Participants assigned to either of the active NT conditions evidenced the longest time to remission, but the combination of NT and IPT was associated with the highest treatment completion rate (Reynolds et al., 1999). The authors also note that while a main effect of IPT was not found, this may be a result of the relatively small sample size or other features of the protocol.

The second phase of MTLD, MTLD-II, was conducted with adults aged 65 and older who met criteria for major depression. Reynolds and colleagues' study (2006, as described by Miller, 2008) treated these clients with combined IPT and paroxetine; once remitted, they received either continued combination therapy or monotherapy. As a maintenance treatment, combined IPT and paroxetine was not more efficacious than monotherapy; however, those with cognitive dysfunction were less likely to experience a recurrence when receiving maintenance IPT (Miller, 2008).

Many characteristics of IPT make the treatment suitable for individuals in late life. The interpersonal focus of treatment and the problem areas characteristic of IPT have strong relevance to the life changes faced by older adults, while the manualized nature of IPT provides a good treatment structure with a population that may tend to discursiveness. However, the flexibility of IPT may work particularly well for older adults who seek a less structured treatment. Older adults may also benefit from the active stance of the IPT therapist, which may enhance the client's ability to achieve his or her goals in a relatively short period of time.

Specific practical adaptations to the original form of IPT may be necessary to better suit the needs of depressed older adults. First, Sholomskas's group (1983) recommends adjusting the length of the typical 50-minute session depending on the physical needs of the client and his or her ability to stay focused for a full session. Additionally, the clinician and client may need to spend more time on the interpersonal inventory at the start of treatment, given the size and number of generations that make up the client's family, as well as the significance of relationships that may have occurred earlier in the client's life. Delving into past relationships more than is generally indicated in IPT may prove helpful for older adults.

It is also particularly important to take into account the unique needs of the client and his or her ability to change when considering the problem area focus of treatment. The client's potentially limited social network may make it difficult to choose a problem area, especially when the interpersonal deficits focus does not seem like the appropriate fit. In some situations, the clinician may also need to amend his or her typical agenda in favor of one that fits the client's priorities more fully. For example, older adults may be less likely to change long-standing communication styles than younger adults, especially in role disputes work. In this case, it may be more advantageous to use different strategies in improving the client's mood, including working toward greater acceptance of the relationship as it is. The rule of thumb is to focus on the problem area that will lead to the fastest improvement.

The clinician must also consider possible changes in therapeutic techniques that are not specific to IPT and are more relevant to the needs of an older client. These include ensuring the client's faith in the therapist's genuine interest in the client's well-being. For this reason, the use of silence, direct confrontation, and nondirective exploration should be done with care. When working with an elderly client, it may also be necessary to accept gifts—particularly those made by the client himself or herself—or to interpret transference that arises, on occasion. Additionally, identifying treatment gains is especially important when working with older adults, not only to remind them that they are capable of making progress and are in control of their own fate but also to encourage the morale and dedication of the client.

Finally, it is quite often the case that older clients seeking IPT treatment may be experiencing spousal bereavement. Several therapeutic and practical concerns should be considered when treating the spousally bereaved, such as financial changes that have occurred as a result of the loss or changes to the interpersonal inventory that must account for the significance of this death in the presence of other recent losses. Please reference Miller and colleagues' (1994) work on this topic for a thorough review.

Brief IPT for Depressed Mothers of Children Receiving Mental Health Treatment

Swartz and colleagues (2006) conducted a preliminary study of brief IPT for depressed mothers whose children were receiving psychiatric treatment (IPT-MOMS) based on the suggestion that these women are an especially high-risk group who only infrequently seek care for themselves (Kessler et al., 2005, as cited in Swartz et al., 2006). IPT was modified to include one engagement session designed to motivate the mothers to commit to treatment, followed by eight sessions of IPT that focus on relationships with ill children. This adaptation uses motivational interviewing techniques to engage clients and is purposefully shorter in an effort to make commitment to treatment less difficult (Swartz et al, 2006). The authors report that mothers receiving this brief form of IPT demonstrated significant improvement in their depressive symptoms from baseline to posttreatment, suggesting that this may be a beneficial approach for depressed mothers whose children are receiving psychiatric treatment.

This treatment was then tested in a small randomized trial involving 47 depressed mothers whose children were receiving some type of psychiatric treatment (Swartz et al., 2008). After assessments at 3- and 9-month follow-ups, clients receiving IPT-MOMS had lower levels of depression and higher levels of functioning at both follow-up time points than those who received treatment as usual. The children of mothers who received the IPT treatment also reported fewer depressive symptoms at 9-month follow-up, suggesting that children may be indirectly positively affected when their mothers receive treatment. The authors conclude that IPT-MOMS may be a particularly promising treatment for depressed mothers of psychiatrically ill children.

IPT FOR THE TREATMENT OF OTHER MOOD DISORDERS

This section will describe research on the efficacy of IPT adaptations for the treatment of dysthymia and bipolar disorder.

Dysthymia

Within the mood spectrum, individuals with dysthymia have been treated with IPT with mixed results. In addition to the long-term mood symptoms that characterize dysthymia, individuals with this disorder may also suffer from social skills deficits or social withdrawal. Thus, it is not surprising that in a pilot study of clients with dysthymia treated with IPT, Mason, Markowitz, and Klerman (1993) found that interpersonal deficits was assigned as the focus of treatment more often than is typically seen when treating other clients with IPT; in fact, it was assigned as the primary problem area more often than all other treatment foci among the nine study participants. Mason's group found that IPT effectively reduced symptoms of depression and increased overall functioning. Based on this work, and in an effort to target the social skills deficits and chronic mood symptoms of dysthymia, Markowitz (1998) adapted IPT into IPT-D, or IPT for dysthymic disorder.

IPT-D maintains the original format of IPT (Klerman et al., 1984) and the concept of the medical model, which is used to teach the client that he or she has been suffering from dysthymia, not an intrinsically depressive or flawed personality, as is often the belief of these clients. The therapist teaches the client that it is the chronic symptoms of dysthymia that have impeded the attainment of appropriate social skills. In addition, the client learns that improving one's social skills may have an antidepressant effect, quite the opposite of what he or she experienced when remaining socially isolated (Markowitz, 1998). It is hoped that the client will view the treatment period as a role transition in which there is a shift from a chronically dysthymic state to being a well person (Markowitz, 1998). This is sometimes considered an *iatrogenic* role transition, because it is initiated by the clinician (Weissman et al., 2007). The therapist may help the client mourn the loss of his role as a person with dysthymia and emphasizes the client's new role in euthymic state (Markowitz, 1998).

In IPT-D specifically, work is done to identify and normalize the client's emotions and to determine whether they are warranted. Role play is frequently used to increase the client's ability to be assertive (Weissman et al., 2007), especially after gaining a better understanding of his or her feelings and their validity. Finally, continuation or maintenance treatment is typically offered based on the chronic nature of dsythymia (Weissman et al., 2007).

Building on earlier work, the effectiveness of IPT-D was also demonstrated by Steiner and colleagues (1998), who treated clients with dysthymic disorder in community settings with either IPT-D (12 sessions), sertraline, or IPT-D and sertraline combined. Although the percentage of participants responding to IPT alone was not as high as that responding to sertraline or combination treatment (51%, 63%, and 62%, respectively), IPT-D did appear to effectively treat a large number of clients in this study.

Thus, IPT-D alone or in combination with pharmacotherapy appeared to be useful. Further analysis of this data showed that the combination of IPT-D and sertraline not only produces the most marked changes in depressive symptoms but is also the most cost-effective (Browne et al., 2002). However, in a more recent study of individuals with pure dysthymia, clients who received IPT-D alone did not fare as well as those who received sertraline or their combination (Markowitz et al., 2005). Based on reduction of depressive symptoms scores, roughly 35% of those who received IPT-D responded to treatment, as compared to more than 55% of those who received sertraline or combined treatment.

This finding was also supported by a study conducted in Brazil, which compared the use of moclobemide in combination with IPT-D to moclobemide with routine care in a group of 35 adults with dysthymia (de Mello et al., 2001). Clients in both groups improved with treatment, but there was a nonsignificant trend for clients in the IPT combination group to continue to improve after 12 weeks of follow-up. Most notable about this study was the fact that IPT-D was successfully conducted in Portuguese and applied to Brazilian clients, supporting the use of IPT in a variety of cultures. The findings presented here suggest that IPT-D may be beneficial for the treatment of dysthymia, but the most effective strategy may be combination treatment.

Bipolar Disorder

For the treatment of bipolar disorder, IPT has been adapted into interpersonal and social rhythm therapy (IPSRT; Frank, 2005). While maintaining the structure, format, and underlying interpersonal focus of IPT, IPSRT adds a social rhythm component to IPT as it was originally developed. The purpose of this component is to assist individuals with bipolar disorder in organizing and maintaining regular social routines or rhythms, with the rationale that instability in daily routines may, in turn, precipitate the disruption in circadian rhythms that has been implicated in the development of manic and depressive episodes (Frank, 2005). As such, clients focus on regulating their daily activities and sleep-wake schedules and managing their medications, while also making efforts to improve their current interpersonal difficulties.

In a 2005 study, Frank and colleagues compared the efficacy of four treatment sequences in combination with medication in a group of 175 clients with bipolar I disorder or schizoaffective disorder, manic type. The four treatment sequences were: acute and maintenance IPSRT, acute and maintenance intensive clinical management (ICM), acute IPSRT and maintenance ICM, and acute ICM and maintenance IPSRT. Although there were no significant differences between the treatments with regard to time to stabilization, after controlling for potentially confounding variables, those who received IPSRT in the acute phase survived longer without a new episode in the maintenance phase, regardless of which maintenance treatment they received (Frank et al., 2005). It is unlikely that this effect is simply a function of the longer IPSRT session, as social rhythm stabilization mediated the effect of longer survival with IPSRT ($p < 0.05$).

IPSRT was also studied as one of the three intensive psychosocial treatments in the Systematic Treatment Enhancement Program for Bipolar Disorder (STEP-BD), in addition to family-focused treatment (FFT) and cognitive–behavioral therapy (CBT). Roughly half of the 293 participants with bipolar I or II depression were assigned to one of these intensive treatments, while the other half was assigned to collaborative care (CC), a brief psychoeducational intervention (Miklowitz, Otto, Frank, Reilly-Harrington, Wisniewski, et al., 2007). All clients also received pharmacotherapy. Those in the intensive psychotherapy cells were eligible to receive up to 30 weekly (median = 13) and biweekly sessions over 9 months, while those in CC received 3 sessions over 6 weeks. Participants in the intensive psychosocial treatments demonstrated better rates of recovery and more rapid times to recovery than those in CC (Miklowitz, Otto, Frank, Reilly-Harrington, Wisniewski, et al., 2007). Although there were no significant differences among the three intensive treatments with regard to time to recovery, the authors report that the study was underpowered to detect such findings. Post hoc univariate comparisons showed that IPSRT was significantly superior to CC, as was FFT.

A more specific analysis of these clients aimed to identify the impact of the intensive psychosocial interventions on functional outcomes after 9 months of treatment (Miklowitz, Otto, Frank, Reilly-Harrington, Kogan, et al., 2007). Participants who received one of the three intensive psychosocial treatments reported more improvement with respect to relationship functioning and satisfaction with life compared to those in CC, and these improvements superseded any changes expected simply from an improvement in mood (Miklowitz, Otto, Frank, Reilly-Harrington, Kogan, et al., 2007). Thus, intensive psychosocial intervention, including IPSRT, appears to be an effective treatment strategy for improving relationship functioning and life satisfaction in individuals with bipolar depression.

IPSRT has also been considered for use as a monotherapy for clients with bipolar II disorder (BPII), based on the potential side effects associated with pharmacotherapy available for bipolar disorders and the fact that individuals with BPII face challenges that may be appropriately addressed by psychotherapy (Swartz, Frank, Frankel, Novick, & Houck, 2009). Within a proof of concept study, individuals with BPII currently depressed were given 12 weeks of IPSRT, which may have been supplemented with pharmacotherapy if the client did not respond (Swartz et al., 2009). The psychoeducation portion of treatment was amended to reflect concerns surrounding BPII, rather than BPI. The study demonstrated the feasibility of treating depression in BPII with IPSRT alone based on the improvements in depressive and manic symptoms and in overall illness severity (Swartz et al., 2009).

IPSRT has also been adapted for use with adolescents with bipolar spectrum disorders (Hlastala & Frank, 2006). Interpersonal interventions, adapted according to IPT-A (Mufson, Dorta, Moreau, & Weissman, 2004), focus on current interpersonal issues that are significant areas of concern and importance during adolescence. A shorter, teen friendly Social Rhythm Metric for Adolescents (SRM-A; see Hlastala & Frank, 2006) is used, based on the five-item SRM (Monk, Frank, Potts, & Kupfer, 2002), with three items added to promote healthy adolescent behaviors. As well, interventions to target school functioning were added, which include creating a consistent school schedule, communicating with school personnel regarding bipolar disorder and relevant needs for accommodations or behavioral support, coaching the adolescent regarding school issues, and evaluating/revising expectations regarding school functioning in the context of having a mental illness. When relevant, family members may participate in family psychoeducation sessions. Parents are also encouraged to be involved in additional therapy sessions depending on the cognitive/social developmental level and or clinical acuity of the adolescent and/or if the interpersonal problem area chosen as the focus of treatment was interpersonal disputes with the parents. An in-depth review of the developmental modifications can be found in Hlastala and Frank (2006).

Hlastala, Kottler, McClellan, and McCauley (2010) recently completed an open trial of Interpersonal and Social Rhythm Therapy for Adolescents (IPSRT-A) in adolescents (ages 13–18) diagnosed with a bipolar spectrum disorder. Twelve adolescents participated in 16 to 18 sessions of adjunctive IPSRT-A over 20 weeks. Results from this open trial indicate that IPSRT-A shows promise as an effective adjunctive psychosocial treatment for adolescents with bipolar disorder. At the end of the 20-week treatment course of IPSRT-A, participants experienced significant improvement in general psychiatric symptomatology, manic and depressive symptoms, and global functioning when compared to pretreatment. Feasibility and acceptability of IPSRT-A were also high. Currently, a randomized controlled trial is underway to examine effects of adjunctive IPSRT-A compared to treatment as usual on psychiatric symptoms and psychosocial functioning in bipolar adolescents ages 12 to 19 (S. Hlastala, personal communication, December 17, 2008).

IPT FOR THE TREATMENT OF OTHER MENTAL HEALTH DISORDERS

In this section we outline the research describing the efficacy of IPT when used to treat anxiety disorders, personality disorders, substance abuse, and eating disorders.

Anxiety Disorders

IPT has been modified for the treatment of anxiety or for the treatment of depressed clients with comorbid anxiety and has been explored in a number of preliminary research studies. The utility of IPT for clients with panic disorder is somewhat unclear. One study of the treatment of clients with major depression with and without comorbid anxiety disorders using

IPT or nortriptyline reported that those with anxiety disorders demonstrate poorer recovery than those without (Brown, Schulberg, Madonia, Shear, & Houck, 1996). Likewise, in a study identifying predictors of acute response to IPT in 134 depressed women, Feske and colleagues (1998) found that those who did not remit were more likely to have a diagnosis of lifetime panic disorder and reported higher levels of current somatic anxiety. They argued that somatic anxiety symptoms may be a "soft sign" of a panic disorder diathesis, or they may be expressed as fear in response to an unfamiliar sensation. Thus, there is some suggestion that treatment of panic symptoms with IPT may prove to be challenging.

Similarly, a 2000 study conducted by our group (Frank, Shear, et al., 2000) demonstrated that depressed women who reported higher levels of lifetime panic-agoraphobic symptoms, as measured by the Panic-Agoraphobic Spectrum Assessment, Self-Report (PAS-SR; Cassano et al., 1999; Shear, Rucci, Grochocinski, Vanderbilt, & Houck, 2001), were less likely to respond to IPT and took longer to remit.

In response to these findings, Cyranowski et al. (2005) designed a pilot study to test the use of an adaptation of interpersonal psychotherapy for individuals whose depression is complicated by panic symptoms (IPT-PS). This treatment was modified from original IPT by providing psychoeducation regarding anxiety symptoms; adding some cognitive–behavioral strategies, including providing psychoeducation regarding anxiety symptoms; targeting avoidance behaviors; identifying emotions; increasing assertiveness; and addressing distress related to separation from significant others. The study did not include a control group and included the possibility of pharmacotherapy for those who did not remit with IPT-PS alone; yet the results demonstrate improvement among the clients receiving IPT-PS (Cyranowski et al., 2005).

Similarly, in a recent study Lipsitz and colleagues (2006) utilized a modified version of IPT for panic disorder (IPT-PD), a key strategy of which is that the therapist strongly links the client's panic symptoms and his or her interpersonal situation. The researchers found that IPT may be effective in the treatment of panic disorder. Additionally, this group utilized IPT for the treatment of social anxiety disorder (SAD; Lipsitz et al., 2008), given the interpersonal context of SAD. Part of this modification included the transformation of the interpersonal deficits problem area to a "therapeutic role transition" problem area in which the acknowledgement of SAD as a treatable disorder enables the client to experience a role change (Lipsitz et al., 2008). Similar to IPT work in the treatment of dysthymia, the client leaves behind the view of himself or herself as an internally flawed person in favor of viewing himself or herself as someone with a treatable disorder. In this modification, Lipsitz and colleagues (2008) explain that "a temperamental predisposition interacts with early and later life experiences to initiate and maintain SAD" (p. 544). The 2008 study randomized 70 clients with SAD to 14 sessions of IPT-SP or supportive therapy. Contrary to their hypothesis, the authors found that IPT was not associated with benefits above and beyond those of supportive therapy, although clients in both groups did experience a decrease in SAD symptoms. The authors note that the clients may have benefited from a longer course of IPT. Lipsitz and colleagues also suggest that perhaps IPT is better suited for the treatment of disorders that have a more recent or more acute onset, as opposed to disorders that are typically more chronic, such as SAD.

Utilizing the Lipsitz, Markowitz, and Cherry (1997) treatment manual for IPT for social phobia, Borge and colleagues (2008) conducted a study of IPT for the treatment of severe social phobia in a residential setting (RIPT). Eighty Norwegian participants were selected from a residential treatment clinic and assigned to approximately 68 hours of RIPT or residential cognitive therapy (RCT) in both group and individualized settings, although most were in a group setting. RIPT treatment integrated aspects from manuals of both group IPT (Wilfley et al., 2000) and IPT-SP (Lipsitz et al., 1997). As a manual for group CT was not available, they developed their own group residential modification for RCT. Borge and colleagues reported no difference between the treatments on clients' reported social phobia either at posttreatment or at a 1-year follow-up, although the social exposure available via the group therapy setting in both treatment conditions may have confounded the actual treatments.

While the majority of treatments for posttraumatic stress disorder (PTSD) involve exposure to stimuli that are reminders of a traumatic event, some preliminary work has been done on the use of IPT for the treatment of PTSD. Bleiberg and Markowitz (2005) conducted a pilot study in

14 adults with PTSD who were treated with 14 weeks of IPT, which had a particular focus on the interpersonal sequelae of trauma. While there was no control group in this study, the authors report that all clients receiving IPT reported a reduction in their PTSD symptoms; almost 40% of clients achieved remission, and almost 70% responded to treatment. The authors suggest that exposure to stimuli related to a past traumatic event may not be a necessary component of successful treatment of PTSD.

More recently, researchers in Australia conducted an open trial of group IPT for PTSD (Robertson et al., 2007). This modification is described by Robertson, Rushton, Bartrum, and Ray (2004). Findings suggest that those who completed treatment experienced a moderate improvement in some PTSD symptoms, as well as psychological distress and depressive symptoms. Thus, the evidence supporting the efficacy of IPT for the treatment of PTSD is somewhat limited and future studies are needed. Nonetheless, there is some suggestion that a modified form of IPT, in individual or group format, may be helpful for some clients suffering from anxiety disorders.

Personality Disorders

The treatment of clients with personality disorders or with personality pathology that is secondary to depression has also been investigated using IPT. Several studies have investigated the impact of personality disorders on the treatment of depression (e.g., Zuckerman, Prusoff, Weissman, & Padian, 1980) and the ways in which they may co-occur and even complicate each other (Thase, 1996).

In a study of individuals with depression who were treated with IPT, Bearden, Lavelle, Buysse, Karp, and Frank (1996) showed that those with comorbid personality pathology were less likely to respond to the treatment, while those who did respond experienced a longer time to remission than those without personality pathology. A more recent study of IPT-M for women with depression showed that those with personality pathology reported higher rates of recurrence after their depression initially remitted (41% vs. 20%) and a shorter time to recurrence than those without personality pathology (Cyranowski et al., 2004). Prior to this, findings from the National Institute of Mental Health Treatment of Depression

Collaborative Research Program (NIMH TDCRP; Shea et al., 1990) showed a nonsignificant trend for a smaller reduction of depressive symptoms among clients with personality disorders than those with depression only.

In spite of the complications that accompany comorbid personality pathology, there is some suggestion that IPT-M may lead to a reduction of personality pathology in those who previously achieve a remission of their depression (Cyranowski et al., 2004). In this study of maintenance treatments for depressed women, features of personality pathology decreased significantly among women who completed 1 and 2 years of maintenance IPT treatment without suffering a recurrence of depression. However, the authors note that perhaps these findings do not reflect a change in personality pathology so much as a reemergence of the individual's normal, nondepressed personality. Still, the authors argue that there is a significant change in "personality disorder-like" symptoms as a result of treatment.

More recently, Markowitz, Skodol, and Bleiberg (2006) recommended the use of IPT to treat borderline personality disorder (BPD). The authors note that IPT may be particularly appropriate for the treatment of this group because of the interpersonal nature of the problems experienced by those with BPD, which may be improved by focusing on social dysfunction. Some features of this adaptation include an awareness of termination issues throughout the course of treatment (based on the separation difficulties that often plague clients with BPD), increasing treatment length, and focusing on the chronicity of the disorder, suicidal behavior risk, and potential difficulty in securing an alliance.

Markowitz, Skodol, and Bleiberg's (2006) claim was supported by a recent study comparing IPT and CBT as treatments for individuals with depression and BPD, in which 32 individuals received IPT plus pharmacotherapy or CBT plus pharmacotherapy for 24 weeks (Bellino et al., 2007). The authors report that there was no difference between groups in the proportions of clients who achieved remission from depression, but those who received IPT showed more improvement in social functioning and the domineering or controlling and intrusive or needy domains of the Inventory of Interpersonal Problems (Horowitz, Rosenberg, Baer, Ureño, & Villaseñor, 1998).

Although the findings described here present mixed results as to the efficacy of IPT for clients with depression and comorbid personality disorders, changes in personality pathology may occur as a result of a longer course of treatment and when IPT is conducted in a maintenance setting with an increased focus on long-term, characterological difficulties.

Substance Abuse

While there has been much interest in using IPT for clients who report substance abuse, this application has proven relatively difficult, perhaps because of difficulties in recruiting participants (Rounsaville, Glazer, Wilber, Weissman, & Kleber, 1983). Early on, Rounsaville and colleagues (1985) described the modification of IPT for individuals with cocaine abuse as a short-term and focused treatment that would emphasize a medical model (with the use of pharmacotherapy), a focus on the client's interpersonal challenges, and the therapist's explorative and supportive stance. The authors note that the goals of this treatment are abstinence from cocaine use and improving strategies for combating the interpersonal problems that are associated with the substance use. In this way, the authors explain the rationale for using an interpersonal treatment for this population, as it seems that a large component of the substance use may be associated with or may be predicted by interpersonal problems.

While their original description was intended for the treatment of cocaine abuse, it seems likely that these treatment modifications may be appropriate for clients abusing other substances. However, treatment with this population is still difficult, both in terms of high drop-out rates of participants and the fact that IPT was less successful at treating study participants than other active treatments (Carroll et al., 1991; Carroll et al., 2004).

More recently, Markowitz, Kocsis, Christos, Bleiberg, and Carlin (2008) investigated the effectiveness of IPT-D as compared to brief supportive therapy (BSP) for 26 individuals with dysthymic disorder and alcohol abuse. Clients in both groups reported a decrease in depressive symptoms and an increase in alcohol abstinence. The IPT group demonstrated greater improvement in depressive symptoms, but neither group improved significantly on measures of alcohol use. Thus, while IPT-D does not effectively treat alcohol abuse, the presence of alcohol abuse in dysthymic clients does not interfere with effective treatment of depressive symptoms. Overall, we see relative difficulty in using IPT to treat clients with substance abuse problems.

Eating Disorders

In contrast, IPT has been used quite successfully in the treatment of eating disorders. In a 1991 study Fairburn and colleagues treated 75 clients with bulimia nervosa with IPT, behavior therapy (BT), or CBT. IPT performed as well as CBT at improving the frequency of overeating, depressive symptoms, and social functioning. However, the authors concluded that IPT is not as effective as CBT at treating bulimia as it was not able to address some important characteristics of the disorder, such as attitudes toward shape and weight and attempts to diet (Fairburn et al., 1991). Nonetheless, individuals receiving IPT did show improvement after acute treatment and continued to demonstrate improvement in the year following treatment. This effect was described in another report from this study (Fairburn, Jones, Peveler, Hope, & O'Connor, 1993), which found that the differences in efficacy between the two treatments seen during acute treatment disappeared during follow-up. This suggests that IPT may be as effective as CBT, but the treatment may take longer to take effect. This finding may be somewhat surprising given the historical focus on cognitive and behavioral changes (not interpersonal ones) in eating disorders treatment (Fairburn et al., 1993); still, treatment for bulimia nervosa may be successful without focusing directly on the patient's eating habits or attitudes about shape.

In an effort to extend and to better understand the findings of the 1993 study, Agras, Walsh, Fairburn, Wilson, and Kraemer (2000) proposed a project in which 220 clients with bulimia nervosa received CBT or IPT for 20 weeks. Contrary to the earlier findings, this study found that CBT is more beneficial than IPT for clients with this disorder. However, examination of follow-up analyses indicate that the IPT group showed continued improvement after acute treatment while the CBT group showed a slight relapse or did not improve any further during this period. Nonetheless, they argue that these findings support the continued use of CBT for the treatment of bulimia nervosa over and above that of IPT.

In 1993, Wilfley and colleagues conducted a study of group IPT as compared to group CBT and a wait-list condition for 56 females with bulimia nervosa. The authors suggest that the significant reduction of binge eating behaviors in both active treatment groups, which was not found in the wait-list group, supports the role of both eating behavior and interpersonal factors in the treatment of bulimia. Building on these results, Wilfley's group (2002) conducted a study of a modified version of IPT-G as compared to group CBT for the treatment of binge-eating disorder. Participants with binge-eating disorder were randomized to group IPT or CBT, receiving 20 weekly group sessions and 3 individual sessions. The findings suggested that group IPT and CBT are equally effective for the treatment of binge-eating disorder, both after acute treatment and at 1-year follow-up. As with other studies on the effectiveness of IPT for eating disorders, the results have generally shown some improvement among clients receiving IPT, although this improvement may not exceed the effects of CBT.

Finally, the use of IPT for anorexia nervosa has been supported by some (McIntosh, Bulik, McKenzie, Luty, & Jordan, 2000) who note that both IPT and more traditional treatments for the disorder focus on interpersonal and family dysfunction problems as a way of decreasing symptoms of anorexia. McIntosh's group explains that the challenges faced by this group may be "readily conceptualized within the IPT framework" (p. 134).

IPT FOR THE TREATMENT OF CLIENTS WITH MEDICAL CONDITIONS

This section will describe research on the efficacy of IPT for depressed clients with other medical conditions. Information on the use of IPT for those with postpartum depression, comorbid HIV, and other chronic illnesses will be included here.

HIV-Positive Clients

Markowitz and colleagues created a version of IPT that was adapted for the treatment of HIV-seropositive clients with comorbid depression (Markowitz, Klerman, Perry, Clougherty, & Josephs, 1993). In this adaptation, treatment focuses on how to deal with having two medical illnesses (here,

HIV and depression). It is not unlikely that these clients' depression may have developed as a consequence of having an HIV diagnosis and the possibility of a life that may be shortened by the disease. Thus, using this adaptation of IPT, HIV-positive clients are encouraged make the most out of the life they have left.

This modified version of IPT was originally used in a pilot study of 24 depressed clients who were also HIV-seropositive, in which 88% recovered from their depression (Markowitz et al., 1993). Later, these researchers used IPT in a study of 101 HIV-positive clients with depressive symptoms. Using the NIMH TDCRP as a treatment design model, clients were randomly assigned to receive treatment with IPT, CBT, supportive psychotherapy (SP), or imipramine plus SP. Although all groups improved, amelioration of depressive symptoms was significantly greater for participants who received IPT alone or imipramine plus SP than for those who received CBT or SP alone (Markowitz et al., 1998). Thus, IPT may be effective for the treatment of clients with HIV and comorbid depression.

Chronic Illness

In a related area, Schulberg's group (1993) has conducted studies on the efficacy of IPT for clients with a chronic illness who also report comorbid depressive symptoms. These studies were conducted in a primary medical care setting. The researchers note that the role transitions experienced by this group of clients often pertain to the transition from a well person to someone who is chronically ill. Part of the role transition is learning to accept the changes that accompany such a life transition and anticipating future opportunities for growth despite the chronic illness (Schulberg et al., 1993). The authors also observe that problems of unresolved grief in clients with a chronic illness may be associated with somatic symptoms; "the unresolved grief often presents as intense anxiety about serious personal illness or illness in a significant other. The client may then display depressive symptoms, but lack any awareness of their relationship to past unresolved grief" (p. 281). It is possible that exploring unresolved grief experienced by these clients may lead to not only a reduction in depressive symptoms but also a reduction in some somatic symptoms that are related to the depression.

Other researchers have suggested the use of IPT for individuals with chronic illnesses because of the inclusion of the medical model and the strategy of giving the client the sick role, which plays an important part in IPT (Koszycki, Lafontaine, Frasure-Smith, Swenson, & Lesperance, 2004). IPT was used in an open pilot study with depressed individuals who also have coronary disease. All participants received IPT, although some also received antidepressant medication. The results suggest that IPT may be a beneficial treatment for depressed clients with coronary disease based on a significant reduction of depressive symptoms and the fact that more than half of the participants achieved remission by the end of the study (Koszycki et al., 2004). As it is unclear whether these results may be due to the effect of study medications, further testing with a control group is warranted.

More recently, a group of Canadian researchers conducted a study on the effects of pharmacotherapy and IPT on depressed clients who also have coronary artery disease, called the Canadian Cardiac Randomized Evaluation of Antidepressant and Psychotherapy Efficacy (CREATE) Trial (Lesperance et al., 2007). In the psychosocial intervention arm of this study, clients were randomized to 12 weekly sessions of IPT plus clinical management (CM) or CM only. Those who received combination treatment received IPT followed immediately by a CM session. Despite previous success using IPT with this population, this study's findings suggest no added value of IPT over CM. However, the severity of depression in this group (24-item Hamilton scores of 20 or greater) may have had an effect on the outcome. Overall, it appears that in some contexts IPT may have an effect on depressive symptoms experienced by clients with a chronic illness; further research investigating this effect is recommended.

SPECIFIC PROBLEMS AND CLIENT POPULATIONS WHERE THE IPT APPROACH IS AND IS NOT EFFECTIVE

With a few exceptions, IPT as modified for the treatment of specific disorders has proven to be successful. Some results have been mixed when IPT has been used for clients with anxiety disorders (e.g., Brown et al., 1996), chronic illnesses (e.g., Koszycki et al., 2004), and substance abuse and dependence (e.g., Carroll et al., 1991; Rounsaville et al., 1983) and in depressed clients with personality pathology (e.g., Bearden et al., 1996; Cyranowski et al., 2004). Yet, even these mixed findings suggest that future work should continue to investigate the use of IPT for these populations and to further modify IPT for more successful treatment of these disorders.

HOW DOES IPT WORK WITH CLIENTS FROM DIVERSE CULTURAL BACKGROUNDS?

Studies on the efficacy of IPT have shown that the treatment can be successfully used with diverse clients (e.g., Grote, Bledsoe, Swartz, & Frank, 2004). In the study described above, Markowitz and colleagues specifically tested the effect of the ethnicity-psychotherapy interaction on treatment outcome (Markowitz, Spielman, Sullivan, & Fishman, 2000). They found that African Americans who received CBT reported poorer outcomes than other clients in this treatment cell; however, African Americans and other clients in the IPT treatment group fared equally well.

Moreover, the use of IPT with a diverse population seems to require few modifications, similar to the adaptations that would be necessary with any other type of psychotherapy. Markowitz and Swartz (2007) note that while taking a detailed history and completing the interpersonal inventory "therapists can easily use this framework to find out what constitutes 'normal' and 'abnormal' expectations in the client's culture" (p. 229). Overall, it is necessary to take cultural norms into account when conceptualizing treatment with all clients, although using IPT with diverse populations seems to require a limited number of adaptations, if any. Below are descriptions of the applicability in widely diverse cultures.

Group IPT in Uganda (IPT-GU)

Verdeli and colleagues (2003) described the use of group IPT for individuals in rural Uganda. The authors explain that this population is particularly suited for such a treatment based on the high prevalence of the HIV epidemic in that area, the high rate of depressive symptoms reported by these individuals and their family members (often as a consequence of the illness of their relatives), and the difficulty in treating depression because of the dearth of doctors and the high cost of medication. They hypothesized that a time-limited psychosocial treatment may be beneficial for depressed individuals in this community. Verdeli's group also noted the importance of testing the applicability of IPT in a non-Western culture that is quite different than the one in which the psychotherapy was initially designed. This modification of IPT is quite similar to the original structure of the treatment, but it was simplified for use by nonclinicians and the format's flexibility was increased to accommodate lifestyle differences of this community.

This research group examined both the feasibility of implementing this treatment in a rural African setting and the efficacy of IPT in treating this population (Bolton et al., 2003). Individuals from 30 rural African villages who reported depressive symptoms were treated with group IPT or treatment as usual (TAU), which consisted of treatment by local healers, no treatment, or, rarely, hospitalization (Verdeli et al., 2003). Participants were grouped by village into 15 groups of men and 15 groups of women, half of which were assigned to the IPT condition. Treatment groups were led by local individuals who had learned to conduct IPT during a 2-week intensive training course, providing evidence that local individuals could be successfully trained to effectively lead IPT-GU (Bolton et al., 2003). Those receiving IPT demonstrated a greater reduction in depressive symptoms, in overall symptom severity, in the proportion of participants diagnosed with depression, and in the participants' level of dysfunction than those receiving TAU. The authors conclude that not only is this version of IPT-G effective at reducing depressive symptoms among this rural Ugandan population, but that conducting this type of study and implementing a Western treatment in this setting is quite feasible.

IPT for Depressed Adolescents in a Rural Mental Health Setting

Bearsley-Smith and colleagues (2007) also identified the importance of studying the effectiveness feasibility of IPT for depressed adolescents in a rural mental health service. The authors note that while IPT has been identified as effective for treating depressed urban adolescents, those seen in a rural mental health service often present with more severe depression complicated by comorbid disorders and may face limited available mental health treatment. Thus, this research group is currently conducting a study of 60 adolescents in rural Victoria, Australia, who will receive either 12 weeks of IPT-A or treatment as usual (TAU). The purpose of this study is to determine which treatment yields a greater decrease in depressive symptoms, as well as to assess the feasibility of implementing IPT in a rural mental health setting.

IPT-B for Perinatal Depression in Low-Income Clients

In addition to the deleterious effects of postpartum depression, depression during pregnancy can also have negative effects on both mother and child. Grote, Bledsoe, Swartz, and Frank (2004) identified the need for a psychotherapeutic treatment intended for depressed pregnant women who are looking for an alternative to pharmacotherapy. The authors note that low-income African American and Caucasian urban women are at a much higher risk of developing perinatal depression than their middle-class counterparts, so a form of IPT is needed for this group. Grote and colleagues note that the treatment should be brief, both because of the high drop-out rate among these clients who find it difficult to attend many treatment sessions and because a shorter treatment motivates more efficient achievement of goals. This is particularly relevant to perinatal depression as women are typically motivated to feel well before the birth of their baby.

Therefore, Grote and colleagues (2004) suggest the use of a culturally relevant form of brief IPT (IPT-B) for the optimal treatment of this population. This approach maintains the majority of the original form of IPT but is shortened to eight sessions, and the interpersonal deficits problem area is omitted as resolving depression in this context typically takes more time than allowed in eight sessions. Treatment focuses on building upon a client's strengths rather than attempting to make major life changes based on long-standing pathology. Grote and colleagues also note that the use of homework is encouraged in IPT-B to support a client's progress outside of session. The culturally relevant aspects of this treatment focus on a pretreatment engagement strategy with psychoeducation, reduced burden for this population via shorter treatment duration, delivery of treatment in the client's ob/gyn clinic or over the phone, and assistance in obtaining social services. The use of IPT-B with attention to cultural relevance is predicted to target some of the treatment difficulties typically faced by low-income African American and Caucasian pregnant women.

This research group conducted a pilot study of IPT-B for this population to test whether the treatment could meet the needs of this group of women, following an IPT format described above (Grote et al., 2004). After completion of the acute trial, the clients received six monthly maintenance sessions of IPT. Although this study did not include a control group, the findings suggest that those clients who completed the IPT-B sessions showed a significant improvement in their depressive symptoms both at posttreatment and 6 months postpartum.

More recently, this group conducted a trial of IPT-B and enhanced usual care for the treatment of perinatal depression in low-income women (Grote et al., 2009). The experimental treatment included an engagement session, eight sessions of IPT-B, and up to 6 months of maintenance IPT sessions. Clients receiving enhanced usual care were encouraged to seek treatment at the behavioral health center in the ob/gyn clinic where they were receiving services. In addition, research staff contacted these individuals every 3 weeks to assess mood and to encourage them to enter treatment. The findings show that, as compared to clients randomized to enhanced usual case, those receiving IPT-B showed greater reductions in depression diagnoses and depression symptoms before childbirth and 6 months postpartum, and they showed improvements in social functioning at 6 months postpartum (Grote et al., 2009). Thus, it appears that IPT-B is both a feasible and efficacious treatment for reducing depressive symptoms.

As this relatively long description of adaptations makes clear, IPT has been perceived as a potentially useful treatment for a wide range of clients seeking mental health treatment, including those with anxiety, eating, personality, and substance use disorders. It has also been adapted to different formats and to group settings. With the exception of substance use disorders, the clear majority of these adaptations have indicated, at a minimum, promise and, in many cases, substantial evidence of efficacy.

RESEARCH SUPPORTING THE EFFICACY OF THE IPT APPROACH BASED ON CLIENT CHARACTERISTICS: WHICH CLIENTS ARE LIKELY TO BENEFIT FROM IPT?

In addition to the primary treatment outcome findings of the NIMH TDCRP study, Sotsky and colleagues (1991) examined the effect of a number of client predictors of treatment outcome with IPT. When examining the role of social adjustment, the authors reported that clients with low social dysfunction showed a higher rate of response to IPT than those with high social dysfunction. The authors also found that depressed clients with higher depression severity and higher work dysfunction demonstrated superior response to treatment with IPT (Sotsky et al., 1991). However, this result is based on analyses conducted within individual treatment cells, not across all treatment conditions. Nonetheless, it appears that IPT treats individuals with more severe depression and less functional work abilities quite effectively.

In this chapter we aimed to provide the reader with a thorough description of the efficacy of IPT for the treatment of a variety of disorders and client groups, as well as of the adaptability of IPT for use in novel settings and for challenging psychological problems. Chapter 6 will continue our discussion of recent adaptations to IPT and will review how the treatment may be used successfully in the future.

6

Future Developments

Given the past success of interpersonal psychotherapy (IPT) at treating depression and other disorders, we are encouraged that future work to develop and implement modifications of IPT will prove beneficial for a group of clients that is rapidly increasing in size and diversity. This chapter highlights some of the most recent work that is currently being conducted involving IPT, as described by the researchers who are conducting it. It provides an account of new developments in this area.

Some of this work attempts to implement "classic" IPT in novel settings, while other work involves the modification of IPT for unique populations or in a unique format. Some of these trials investigate the feasibility and acceptance of new adaptations, while those focused on more established models of IPT currently focus on the specificity of the treatment for various populations. New developments in this area also highlight the use of preventative IPT for at-risk groups and others describe efforts to define a link between the symptoms of a disorder and the client's interpersonal dysfunction. Readers will note the geographically and ethnically diverse group of researchers involved in this area of study. This burgeoning work speaks to the appeal and flexibility of IPT, its applicability to a wide range of client populations, and its ease of use among a variety of practitioners.

ADAPTATIONS OF IPT TO OTHER DISORDERS

IPT for the Prevention of Excessive Weight Gain (IPT-WG)

IPT has recently been developed for the prevention of excessive weight gain (IPT-WG) in adolescents who report loss of control eating (LOC) patterns. Common among youth, LOC eating is associated with distress and overweight (Tanofsky-Kraff, 2008) and predicts excessive weight gain over time (Tanofsky-Kraff et al., in press). In theory, LOC eating is believed to be a marker of risk for the development of subsequent clinical eating pathology, such as binge eating disorder (BED). To address this challenge, IPT-WG makes use of both IPT for the prevention of depression in adolescents (IPT Adolescent Skills Training [IPT-AST]; Young, Mufson, & Davies, 2006) and group IPT for BED (Wilfley et al., 2000). This adaptation also evolved from the outcome data of psychotherapy trials for the treatment of BED, which found, unexpectedly, that individuals with the disorder who cease to binge eat tend to maintain their body weight during and/or following treatment (Agras et al., 1995; Agras, Telch, Arnow, Eldredge, & Marnell, 1997; Devlin et al., 2005; Wilfley et al., 1993; Wilfley et al., 2002). It is hypothesized that treatment of LOC eating among youth may reduce excessive weight gain and prevent full-syndrome eating disorders (Tanofsky-Kraff et al., 2007).

IPT-WG for adolescents (12- to 17-year-olds) is delivered in a group of 4–6 members and maintains the key components of traditional IPT. This adaptation was developed specifically to address the particular needs of adolescent girls at high risk for adult obesity by virtue of above-average body mass indices and reports of LOC eating behaviors. IPT-WG focuses on psychoeducation, communication analysis, role playing, and teaching interpersonal communication skills (Young & Mufson, 2003). During the interpersonal inventory, a "closeness circle" (Mufson, Dorta, Moreau, et al., 2004) is used to identify the significant relationships of the participant. Based on IPT for BED, IPT-WG maintains focus throughout the program on linking negative affect to LOC eating, times when individuals eat in response to cues other than hunger, and overconcern about shape and weight (Wilfley et al., 2000). Further, a timeline of personal eating and weight-related problems and life events is discussed individually with participants prior to the group program (M. Tanofsky-Kraff, personal communication, December 11, 2008).

Preventative IPSRT-A

Based on the apparent promise of Interpersonal and Social Rhythm Therapy for Adolescents (IPSRT-A) for those already diagnosed with bipolar disorder (Hlastala & Frank, 2006), a group of researchers from the University of Pittsburgh and the University of Washington has begun a trial investigating the effect of IPSRT-A as a *preventative* treatment for adolescents at risk for bipolar disorder. The rationale for this trial is based in part on numerous studies indicating that poor sleep and social rhythm regulation, particularly during periods of stress, are associated with the onset of mania and depression in vulnerable individuals. Given that adolescence is a period characterized by significant alterations in social routines and sleep/wake patterns and that it is a key developmental stage for illness onset, this period may prove an optimal time for a preventative intervention targeting stabilization of social rhythms for those at risk for developing bipolar disorder.

Research indicates that the single most potent risk factor for the development of bipolar disorder is a positive family history of the illness. Therefore, we (Goldstein, Frank, Axelson, and Birmaher, at the University of Pittsburgh, and Hlastala at the University of Washington) are conducting an open pilot treatment development trial examining an adaptation of IPSRT (Frank, 2005; Hlastala & Frank, 2006) as a preventative intervention for adolescents at high risk for bipolar disorder by virtue of a first-degree relative with the illness. Treatment modifications are designed to target the unique needs of an at-risk population and include abbreviating treatment length and incorporating motivational strategies. Data are being collected to assess change in symptoms, sleep, energy, and psychosocial functioning. The intervention appears to be feasible, and early cases suggest that IPSRT treatment focusing on stabilizing daily rhythms and interpersonal relationships may be beneficial for adolescents at risk for bipolar disorder (T. Goldstein, personal communication, December 8, 2008).

Family-Based IPT

Preadolescent depression increases the risk for recurrent depression into adolescence and adulthood, particularly with a strong family loading for depression. A family-focused, developmentally appropriate modification of IPT has been conceptualized and recently piloted for depressed preadolescents and their parents (see Dietz, Mufson, Irvine, & Brent, 2008). IPT provides a unique treatment framework for addressing distressing interpersonal situations in the family and teaching both preadolescents and parents more effective communication and problem-solving strategies, which may reduce interpersonal distress related to relapse.

Although family-based interpersonal psychotherapy (FB-IPT) adheres to the structure and guiding principles of IPT-A, the problem areas have been expanded to reflect the family or developmental context and to facilitate the dyadic discussion of the effect of interpersonal stressors on mood and depressive symptoms. FB-IPT has also been modified by: (a) increasing the number of conjoint parent sessions and dyadic sessions; (b) using narrative techniques; and (c) increasing graded interpersonal experiments for clients with comorbid anxiety disorders.

An open treatment trial has been conducted to evaluate the feasibility, acceptability, and clinical outcomes of FB-IPT with a sample of depressed preadolescent outpatients (Dietz et al., 2008). Parents chose whether their preadolescents received FB-IPT only or FB-IPT with antidepressant medication, and combination treatment was more strongly favored by parents whose children also had a comorbid anxiety disorder. FB-IPT was associated with high treatment compliance rates (88%); clients who received FB-IPT only were as likely as those receiving FB-IPT and medication to have significant reductions in depressive symptoms and anxiety symptoms and to experience significant improvement in global functioning. Further research on FB-IPT is needed to establish its efficacy as compared to usual outpatient treatment, its use by child clinicians with varying levels of training, and its use in adequately powered randomized controlled trials that can detect group differences (L. Dietz, personal communication, January 6, 2009).

Group IPT for Women Prisoners With Comorbid Substance Use and Major Depression

IPT is particularly pertinent to the treatment needs of incarcerated women with co-occurring depressive disorder (DD) and substance use disorder (SUD) because many of their needs are interpersonal in nature. Incarcerated women with DD-SUD face a number of interpersonal difficulties (Substance Abuse and Mental Health Services Administration, 1999; U.S. Department of Justice, 1999) and harmful attachments (Holtfreter & Morash, 2003). The IPT group (IPT-G) treatment used in a study conducted by Johnson and Zlotnick of Brown University was based on a manual adapted from Wilfley and colleagues (2000) to address specific treatment needs of women prisoners, with particular efforts to improve social support both outside and inside the prison.

The group's primary modification of IPT-G for this population is the timing of the sessions. Because many women prisoners serve short sentences (a few months), the treatment schedule needed to be condensed. Women in the groups attend an individual pregroup, midgroup, and postgroup session, as recommended by Wilfley. The 24 group sessions occur three times per week for 8 weeks just prior to women's release. As women are often returning to conflictual and high-risk interpersonal environments, the women also have individual sessions once per week for 6 weeks after release.

The IPT theory of change itself appears to be a natural fit for the issues that women brought to treatment. They spontaneously reported that the personalized, written case formulations linking depressive symptoms to the IPT problem areas (Wilfley et al., 2000) were helpful in organizing their DD-SUD experiences and therapeutic efforts. Common themes of group discussion focused on interpersonal relationships, and the problem area foci also seemed particularly relevant to this group. As in all therapy groups, it was important that the clients felt comfortable, but safety in the group was critical in this setting because the vast majority of women have trauma histories. Finally, the research group worked hard to help women address conflicts within the group. For most of the groups, these conflictual moments provided powerful *in vivo* experiences for learning communications skills, conflict resolution, and ultimately trust. (J. Johnson, personal communication, December 12, 2008).

IPT in Community Mental Health Settings for Depressed Women With Trauma

In community mental health centers, a large segment of those seeking care are depressed women who have extensive trauma histories, including childhood sexual abuse. Depression among this client population has a chronic and treatment-refractory course and is accompanied by other disorders and challenges. IPT was tested among depressed women with sexual abuse histories in a community mental health center. An uncontrolled pilot study suggested that IPT was feasible and beneficial to study participants with significant improvements in depression and psychological functioning (Talbot et al., 2005).

A randomized controlled trial of IPT compared to usual care in a community mental health center (CMHC) is currently underway. In this adaptation four components are added to address the needs of this specific population: an expanded duration of treatment; an interpersonal-patterns problem area; a sociocultural formulation; and an engagement analysis. The term *IPT-Trauma in Community Settings* (IPT-TCS) is used to refer to interpersonal psychotherapy with these four modifications. The expanded treatment duration matches the realities of attendance patterns in a CMHC. Results from the pilot studies indicated that poor treatment participation was strongly influenced by social barriers, especially the stigma of mental health care and shame associated with trauma histories. The engagement analysis uses IPT strategies in initial sessions to help clients overcome barriers to treatment participation. Based on the need to explicitly include cultural factors in treatment formulations with low-income and minority women, the sociocultural formulation is an elaboration of the interpersonal formulation of IPT focused on cultural influences on clients' interpersonal problems and depression. Finally, the interpersonal-patterns problem area is a trauma-specific modification of one of the IPT problem areas to address chronic interpersonal patterns associated with interpersonal trauma (N. Talbot, personal communication, December 17, 2008).

IPT for Women With Depression and Chronic Pain

Depression and chronic pain are highly prevalent, severely disabling, and frequently comorbid, and clients with both conditions respond poorly to treatments for both depression and pain. Yet no psychosocial treatments have been developed and tested for clients with depression and chronic pain. Low-income women are at increased risk for both conditions and likely to present to their primary care or women's health physicians for treatment. A study conducted by Gamble, Giles, Poleshuck, Talbot, and Zlotnick (E. Poleshuck, personal communication, December 12, 2008) was designed to assess feasibility, adherence, and acceptability of interpersonal treatment for depression and pain (IPT-P) for 16 low-income gynecology patients with major depression and chronic pelvic pain.

Treatment accommodations were made to IPT, including a brief form of treatment, with dose of treatment up to eight sessions. Patients were seen in their gynecologist's office and completed the sessions at their own pace in up to 36 weeks. The investigators offered outreach, transportation, child care, flexible scheduling, and phone sessions as needed. Also, they added a "change in healthy self" problem area and they incorporated cognitive–behavioral pain management strategies based on an individual client's treatment goals. Preliminary findings suggest modest improvement in depression, though women may not obtain full remission of their depression following treatment. This group is now comparing IPT and enhanced treatment as usual in a randomized controlled trial for 60 gynecology patients with depression and chronic pelvic pain. Their goal is to implement, evaluate, and disseminate IPT-P for low-income women to reduce the suffering and expense caused by the deleterious impact of comorbid depression and pain.

IPT for Body Dysmorphic Disorder (IPT-BDD)

Body dysmorphic disorder (BDD) is a preoccupation with an imagined or slight defect in appearance that causes clinically significant distress or impairment in social, occupational, or other important areas of functioning. Interpersonal deficits are a frequent problem in BDD (Phillips, 1996); some clients with BDD become extremely socially isolated, even housebound (Phillips & Diaz, 1997; Phillips, McElroy, Keck, Pope, & Hudson,

1993). Although there are few effective treatments for the disorder, IPT offers a promising way to address the concerns of clients with BDD, particularly because studies have shown IPT to be effective for disorders that share similarities with and may be related to BDD (Phillips, 1996; Phillips, McElroy, Hudson, & Pope, 1995).

Pilot testing of an IPT-BDD manual is currently underway, based on which a novel manualized treatment will be developed and evaluated in a future, larger clinical trial. IPT-BDD follows the three phases of standard IPT for depression (Klerman et al., 1984) extended to 19 consecutive weekly sessions. In the initial sessions there is a particular focus on the interpersonal context in which BDD developed and has been maintained. A problem area focus is identified at the end of the initial phase.

The focus of the middle phase of IPT-BDD is on resolving the interpersonal problem area(s) most related to the client's current symptoms. Specific modifications to IPT-BDD focus on the association of BDD with several interpersonal deficits, including: (a) social isolation (Phillips, 1996), (b) poor self-esteem (Phillips, Pinto, & Jain, 2004), (c) lack of assertiveness (Phillips & McElroy, 2000), (d) rejection sensitivity (Phillips, Nierenberg, Brendel, & Fava, 1996), and (e) feelings of ineffectiveness. Three specific changes have been made to address deficits, avoidance, and nonassertiveness: (a) making connections between appearance concerns and social problems and exploring specific suggestions for decreasing social avoidance; (b) focusing on the client–therapist relationship; and (c) integrating selected, highly compatible CBT techniques with IPT.

IPT-BDD also broadens the IPT problem areas. Borrowing from the modification of IPT for dysthymic clients (Markowitz, 1998), for example, the therapist may focus on a therapeutic transition (e.g., from the sick role to a healthier, more adaptive role) that involves the client learning new skills to accompany a more assertive and less avoidant approach to others. The area of grief/loss has also been broadened to incorporate the "loss of the healthy self" (Frank et al., 2005) and "loss of body perfection." The therapist's task is to help the client grieve for these losses. In the transition/termination phase vulnerabilities for relapse are explicitly discussed, and strategies to prevent relapse are identified. Progress is reviewed and treatment gains reinforced (E. Didie, personal communication, December 18, 2008).

As evidenced throughout this chapter, IPT is currently being adapted for use in new settings and for client populations that are likely to benefit from the implementation of an effective treatment. These modifications represent some of the many ways in which IPT is likely to be used in the future.

7

Summary

We hope that we have provided a picture of interpersonal psycho-therapy (IPT) as a short-term, focused psychotherapy that has demonstrated success for the treatment of depression and a number of other psychiatric disorders. More than that, we hope that the information provided here has armed the reader with resources for implementing IPT in clinical practice. The use of therapeutic strategies that stem from the interpersonal school (e.g., Meyer, 1957; Sullivan, 1953) as a means of reducing psychopathology appears to be intuitively understood and embraced by clients and clinicians alike. In addition to providing the knowledge necessary to utilize this treatment modality, our aim has also been to imbue the reader with the notion that psychotherapeutic work based in an interpersonal context will be both beneficial to the client and professionally enriching for the practitioner.

The underlying premise of IPT is the link between interpersonal problems and the development and maintenance of the client's psycho-pathology, as originally developed by Klerman and colleagues (1984) for the treatment of depression. Therapeutic work toward the amelioration of social role disturbances and the improvement of dysfunctional interpersonal strategies may serve to reduce the client's depressive symptoms.

Thus, reduction of the client's depression and improvement of his or her interpersonal situation are the main goals of treatment. While a focus on the client's interpersonal relationships naturally implies exploration into the client's past, previous social bonds become a focus of treatment only inasmuch as they inform the present.

As discussed previously, the development of IPT came as the result of a study conducted by Klerman, Weissman, and colleagues in the 1960s. The work conducted by these researchers was truly groundbreaking, particularly given the state of research on depression and depression treatments at that time. One of the hallmarks of this group's research was the entirely novel intention to provide standardized treatment to all study participants. This meant that clinicians would follow a consistent treatment plan, the implementation of which could be varied slightly according to the needs of each client. Moreover, although IPT has roots in the interpersonal school of psychiatry, the development of the specific IPT strategies and tactics came as a result of observation of expert clinicians' work rather than as a result of constructing a treatment to fit a specific theory of depression. Klerman and Weissman's ability to synthesize what they observed in order to develop a treatment based on what appeared to be successful treatment for clients with depression led to an intervention that has instinctive appeal to clinicians.

A focus of treatment may be significant life events that have occurred recently or those that have occurred in the past but are still unresolved. This is especially true when the events involve the death of a loved one. Likewise, the social support felt by the individual may also play a role in the conceptualization of treatment and the therapist's choice of treatment strategies. This may be particularly important when social support from a significant other is perceived to be lacking.

Work in IPT for major depression typically lasts 16–20 sessions, contributing to its strength as a short-term treatment that is still able to bring about substantial therapeutic improvement. Another advantage of IPT is its flexibility. While work with some clients is conducted in a time-limited fashion, there is the possibility that a client may return for maintenance treatment if this appears warranted. In this way, therapists and clients may tailor treatment to best suit the needs of the individual. Likewise, briefer forms of IPT may be appropriate for difficult-to-engage clients. This flexibility is also seen when IPT is used to treat clients of varying ages and backgrounds and those who present with a range of disorders. Other key characteristics of treatment with IPT include the use of the medical model, the sick role, and psychoeducation.

The IPT therapist takes a warm, supportive, and active stance. Work in treatment represents a collaboration between the therapist and the client. The therapist may act as the expert at times, supporting the client in a "cheerleader" role; however, the client may also exercise preference as to the problem area focus of treatment. The client is expected to demonstrate a commitment to therapy and a willingness to participate actively in treatment. Of course, IPT is also characterized by the use of the four problem areas of treatment, which narrow the focus of therapeutic work and provide a context for the client's interpersonal challenges.

Several of the strategies used in IPT are aimed at exploring the client's experience, through the use of exploration of affect and elicitation of details. Other active strategies used by the IPT therapist may include exploring options or decision analysis, role playing, and communication analysis. While transference is not typically addressed in IPT, the clinician may use the therapeutic relationship as a model for how clients interact with significant others in their lives.

We hope that this monograph has also indicated the applicability of IPT to a range of client populations and disorders. IPT is effective for the treatment of depression, both in acute and maintenance contexts, and for clients of a range of ages. In addition, IPT or modifications thereof have demonstrated efficacy in the treatment for postpartum depression, bipolar disorder, and eating disorders, and in group settings. There have also been some mixed reviews of IPT for the treatment of clients with anxiety, personality disorders, and alexithymia. Nonetheless, we anticipate that continued work on IPT modifications will result in the successful application of IPT to disorders that have historically been more difficult to treat using an interpersonal modality.

Perhaps the most remarkable developments in recent work on IPT include its use as a treatment for diverse communities around the globe and its implementation by individuals native to these cultures. This work has demonstrated that not only does an interpersonal approach to treatment provide relief for varied clients, but the treatment may be effectively put into practice by practitioners from both Western and non-Western cultures. This success speaks to the universality of IPT and its potential for acceptance by a range of individuals who suffer from psychological challenges. Over the past 40 years the mental health field has witnessed the growth and development of IPT and its acceptance as an effective treatment for depression and a number of other disorders. We are confident that psychologists will embrace IPT and recognize its feasibility, acceptability, and utility for clients in clinical practice.

Glossary of Key Terms

ALEXITHYMIA   An emotional disturbance in which the client experiences difficulty identifying, differentiating, and describing feelings and has difficulty differentiating between somatic sensations and emotions (Lanza di Scalea et al., 2006).

COMMUNICATION ANALYSIS   A short-term IPT strategy used to assist the client in identifying where his or her interpersonal communication may go awry in order to improve communication in the future. In communication analysis, the therapist asks the client to recount exactly what was said between the client and another individual to identify the client's maladaptive communication strategies and look for areas of improvement (Weissman et al., 2007).

DECISION ANALYSIS   An IPT strategy in which the therapist helps clients to identify and weigh potential options in a difficult situation in order to make a sound decision. The therapist may also help the client generate new alternatives that may not have been considered previously (Weissman et al., 2007).

DISSOLUTION   One stage of a role dispute in which the relationship has been permanently damaged and resolution does not appear possible (Weissman et al., 2007).

ENCOURAGEMENT OF AFFECT   An IPT strategy in which the therapist encourages the client to explore and express his or her emotion. This not only allows the client to acknowledge previously unrecognized emotions but may also facilitate the acceptance of unchangeable painful emotions.

IMPASSE   One stage of a role dispute in which open communication has ceased and has been replaced by underlying feelings of anger and resentment, but resolution of the dispute still appears possible (Weissman et al., 2007).

INTERPERSONAL DEFICITS   The IPT problem area that focuses on the client's limited and/or inadequate social contacts, feelings of isolation, and potentially chronic depression. Treatment strategies include identifying maladaptive patterns in past social relationships and using the interaction between the client and the therapist as a model for how the client typically interacts with others. These strategies are used to improve the client's ability at forming and maintaining social relationships.

INTERPERSONAL INVENTORY   An assessment conducted at the beginning of treatment in which the therapist and client identify the most significant individuals in the client's past and present life and explore the nature of the client's relationships with these people (Weissman et al., 2007).

INTERPERSONAL PSYCHOTHERAPY (IPT)   A short-term, focused psychotherapy developed by Gerald L. Klerman, Myrna M. Weissman, and collaborators for the treatment of depression (Klerman et al., 1984; Weissman et al., 2000, 2007).

IPT-A   IPT, modified for the treatment of adolescents (Mufson et al., 1993; Mufson, Dorta, Moreau, et al., 2004).

IPT-AG   Group IPT for adolescents (Mufson, Gallagher, et al., 2004).

IPT-B   Brief IPT, shortened to roughly eight sessions. It has been used for the treatment of perinatal depression in low-income clients (Grote et al., 2009).

IPT-D   IPT, modified for the treatment of dysthymia (Markowitz, 1998).

IPT-G   IPT, modified for treatment in a group setting (Wilfley et al., 2000).

IPT-GU   IPT, modified for treatment in a group setting for depressed individuals in rural Uganda (Bolton et al., 2003; Verdeli et al., 2003).

IPT-LL   IPT, modified for the treatment of older adults (IPT for late-life depression; Miller, 2008).

IPT-M   IPT, modified for maintenance treatment (Frank, 1991).

IPT-MOMS   IPT, modified for the treatment of depressed mothers of children in mental health treatment (Swartz et al., 2006, 2008).

IPT-PS   IPT, modified for the treatment of depression with comorbid panic spectrum symptoms (Cyranowski et al., 2005).

IPT-SP   IPT, modified for the treatment of social phobia (Lipsitz et al., 1997).

IPSRT   Interpersonal and social rhythm therapy; adapted from IPT and intended for use with individuals suffering from bipolar disorder (Frank, 2005). IPSRT adds a social rhythm focus that is intended to stabilize the client's daily routines and sleep/wake cycles.

IPSRT-A   IPSRT, modified for the treatment of adolescents (Hlastala & Frank, 2006).

NONRECIPROCAL ROLE EXPECTATIONS   Often identified on the part of the client whose treatment focuses on role disputes; expectations held by the client that are not shared by the other party to the dispute and expectations on the part of the other party to the dispute that are not held by the client.

PROBLEM AREAS   A focus of treatment that links the client's recent interpersonal difficulties with the onset of his or her depression. Assigning a client's depression-related difficulties to one of the four problem areas (unresolved grief, role transition, role dispute, or interpersonal deficits) is one way that the therapist places the client's depression in an interpersonal context and focuses the therapeutic work.

PROVOKING AGENTS   Significant chronic difficulties or discrete events in one's life (Brown & Harris, 1978) that are temporally linked to the onset of depression; in combination with *vulnerability factors*, these may contribute to the development of depression.

RENEGOTIATION   One stage of a role dispute in which differences and problems are acknowledged and openly discussed (Weissman et al., 2007).

ROLE DISPUTES   The IPT problem area in which the source of the client's depression is linked to a dispute with a significant other. The dispute typically centers on a disagreement regarding the conceptualization of the client and/or significant other's social role. Nonreciprocal role expectations often exist between the two individuals involved in the dispute. Treatment strategies typically include development of improved communication, assessment of the current relationship expectations, and negotiation of new expectations with the other party to the dispute (Weissman et al., 2007).

ROLE TRANSITIONS   The IPT problem area in which treatment focuses on difficult changes in the client's social role. Treatment strategies typically include realistic evaluation of the old role, acknowledgment of the role transition as a loss, consideration of the new role in an optimistic light, and identification of positive features of the new role, as well as efforts to aid the client in mastering the new role.

SICK ROLE   A concept created by Parsons (1951) that exempts the client from some social obligations and responsibilities and promotes his or her identification as a person who is in a socially undesirable emotional state, in need of help. This role implies the client's agreement to cooperate with the care provider to work toward getting well.

UNRESOLVED GRIEF   The IPT problem area that focuses on an unresolved reaction to the death of a loved one. Treatment strategies include identifying and recalling memories involving the deceased, experiencing feelings related to those memories, a gradual letting go of past experiences related to the deceased, and movement toward developing new relationships and life experiences.

VULNERABILITY FACTORS   Underlying stresses that, in combination with *provoking agents*, may contribute to the development of depression (Brown & Harris, 1978).

Suggested Readings

Elkin, I., Shea, M. T., Watkins, J. T., Imber, S. D., Sotsky, S. M., Collins, J. F., . . . Parloff, M. B. (1989). National Institute of Mental Health Treatment of Depression Collaborative Research Program. General effectiveness of treatments. *Archives of General Psychiatry, 46*(11), 971–982.

Frank, E. (2005). *Treating bipolar disorder: A clinician's guide to interpersonal and social rhythm therapy.* New York, NY: Guilford Press.

Frank, E., Kupfer, D. J., Perel, J. M., Cornes, C., Jarrett, D. B., Mallinger, L. G., . . . Grochocinski, V. J. (1990). Three-year outcomes for maintenance therapies in recurrent depression. *Archives of General Psychiatry, 47,* 1093–1099.

Hinrichsen, G. A., & Clougherty, K. F. (2006). *Interpersonal psychotherapy for depressed older adults.* Washington, DC: American Psychological Association.

Klerman, G. L., DiMascio, A., Weissman, M. M., Prusoff, B., & Paykel, E. S. (1974). Treatment of depression by drugs and psychotherapy. *American Journal of Psychiatry, 131*(2), 186–191.

Klerman, G. L., & Weissman, M. M. (Eds.). (1993). *New applications of interpersonal psychotherapy.* Washington, DC: American Psychiatric Press.

Klerman, G. L., Weissman, M. M., Rounsaville, B. J., & Chevron, E. S. (1984). *Interpersonal psychotherapy of depression.* New York, NY: Basic Books.

Markowitz, J. C. (1998). *Interpersonal psychotherapy for dysthymic disorder.* Washington, DC: American Psychiatric Press.

Stuart, S., & Robertson, M. (2003). *Interpersonal psychotherapy: A clinician's guide.* New York, NY: Oxford University Press.

Weissman, M. M., Markowitz, J. C., & Klerman, G. L. (2000). *Comprehensive guide to interpersonal psychotherapy.* New York, NY: Basic Books.

Weissman, M. M., Markowitz J. C., & Klerman, G. L. (2007). *Clinician's quick guide to interpersonal psychotherapy.* New York, NY: Oxford University Press.

References

Agras, W. S., Telch, C. F., Arnow, B., Eldredge, K., Detzer, M. J., Henderson, J., . . . Marnell, M. (1995). Does interpersonal therapy help patients with binge eating disorder who fail to respond to cognitive-behavioral therapy? *Journal of Consulting and Clinical Psychology, 63*(3), 356–360.

Agras, W. S., Telch, C. F., Arnow, B., Eldredge, K., & Marnell, M. (1997). One-year follow-up of cognitive–behavioral therapy for obese individuals with binge eating disorder. *Journal of Consulting and Clinical Psychology, 65*(2), 343–347.

Agras, W. S., Walsh, T., Fairburn, C. G., Wilson, G. T., & Kraemer, H. C. (2000). A multicenter comparison of cognitive–behavioral therapy and interpersonal psychotherapy for bulimia nervosa. *Archives of General Psychiatry, 57*, 459–466.

Alem, A., Pain, C., Araya, M., & Hodges, B. D. (in press). Co-creating a psychiatry resident program with Ethiopians, for Ethiopians, in Ethiopia: The Toronto Addis Ababa Psychiatry Project (TAAPP). *Academic Psychiatry*.

Aneshensel, C. S., & Stone, J. D. (1982). Stress and depression: A test of the buffering model of social support. *Archives of General Psychiatry, 39*(12), 1392–1396.

Bearden, C., Lavelle, N., Buysse, D., Karp, J. F., & Frank, E. (1996). Personality pathology and time to remission in depressed outpatients treated with interpersonal psychotherapy. *Journal of Personality Disorders, 10*(2), 164–173.

Bearsley-Smith, C., Browne, M. O., Sellick, K., Villanueva, E. V., Chesters, J., Francis, K., . . . Reddy, P. (2007). Does interpersonal psychotherapy improve clinical care for adolescents with depression attending a rural child and adolescent mental health service? Study protocol for a cluster randomised feasibility trial. *BMC Psychiatry, 7*(53), 1–7.

Beck, A. T., Rush, A. J., Shaw, B. F., & Emery, G. (1979). *Cognitive therapy of depression.* New York, NY: Guilford.

Bellino, S., Zizza, M., Rinaldi, C., & Bogetto, F. (2007). Combined therapy of major depression with concomitant borderline personality disorder: Comparison of interpersonal and cognitive psychotherapy. *The Canadian Journal of Psychiatry, 52*(11), 718–725.

Bleiberg, K. L., & Markowitz, J. C. (2005). A pilot study of interpersonal psychotherapy for posttraumatic stress disorder. *The American Journal of Psychiatry, 162*(1), 181–183.

Blom, M. B. B., Jonker, K., Dusseldorp, E., Spinhoven, P., Hoencamp, E., Haffmans, J., ... van Dyck, R. (2007). Combination treatment for acute depression is superior only when psychotherapy is added to medication. *Psychotherapy and Psychosomatics, 76,* 289–297.

Bolton, P., Bass, J., Neugebauer, R., Verdeli, H., Clougherty, K. F., Wickramaratne, P., ... Weissman, M. M. (2003). Group interpersonal psychotherapy for depression in rural Uganda: A randomized controlled trial. *Journal of the American Medical Association, 289*(13), 3117–3324.

Borge, F. M., Hoffart, A., Sexton, H., Clark, D. M., Markowitz, J. C., & McManus, F. (2008). Residential cognitive therapy versus residential interpersonal therapy for social phobia: A randomized clinical trial. *Journal of Anxiety Disorders, 822,* 1–20.

Brown, C., Schulberg, H. C., Madonia, M. J., Shear, M. K., & Houck, P. R. (1996). Treatment outcomes for primary care patients with major depression and lifetime anxiety disorders. *The American Journal of Psychiatry, 153*(10), 1293–1300.

Brown, G. W., & Harris, T. (1978). *Social origins of depression: A study of psychiatric disorder in women.* New York, NY: Free Press.

Browne, G., Steiner, M., Roberts, J., Gafni, A., Byrne, C., Dunn, E., ... Kraemer, J. (2002). Sertraline and/or interpersonal psychotherapy for patients with dysthymic disorder in primary care: 6-month comparison with longitudinal 2-year follow-up of effectiveness and costs. *Journal of Affective Disorders, 68,* 317–330.

Brunstein-Klomek, A., & Mufson, L. (2006). Interpersonal psychotherapy for depressed adolescents. *Child and Adolescent Psychiatric Clinics of North America, 15,* 959–975.

Brunstein-Klomek, A., Zalsman, G., & Mufson, L. (2007). Interpersonal psychotherapy for depressed adolescents (IPT-A). *Israel Journal of Psychiatry and Related Sciences, 44*(1), 40–46.

Carroll, K., Fenton, L. R., Ball, S., Nich, C., Frankforter, T., Shi, J., ... Rounsaville, B. J. (2004). Efficacy of disulfiram and cognitive behavior therapy in cocaine-dependent outpatients. *Archives of General Psychiatry, 61,* 264–272.

Carroll, K., Rounsaville, B. J., & Gawin, F. (1991). A comparative trial of psychotherapies for ambulatory cocaine abusers: Relapse prevention and interpersonal psychotherapy. *American Journal of Drug and Alcohol Abuse, 17*(3), 229–247.

Cassano, G. B., Banti, S., Mauri, M., Dell'Osso, L., Miniati, M., Maser, J. D., . . . Rucci, P. (1999). Internal consistency and discriminant validity of the Structured Clinical Interview for Panic-Agoraphobic Spectrum (SCI-PAS). *International Journal of Methods in Psychiatry Research, 8,* 138–145.

Cohen, M. B., Baker, G., Cohen, R. A., Fromm-Reichmann, F., & Weigert, E. V. (1954). An intensive study of twelve cases of manic-depressive psychosis. *Psychiatry, 17*(2), 103–137.

Cornes, C. L., & Frank, E. (1996). Interpersonal psychotherapy. In L. J. Dickstein, J. M. Oldham, & M. B. Riba (Eds.), *Review of psychiatry.* Washington, DC: American Psychiatric Press.

Cyranowski, J. M., Frank, E., Shear, M. K., Swartz, H., Fagiolini, A., Scott, J., . . . Kupfer, D. J. (2005). Interpersonal psychotherapy for depression with panic spectrum symptoms: A pilot study. *Depression and Anxiety, 21,* 140–142.

Cyranowski, J. M., Frank, E., Winter, E., Rucci, P., Novick, D., Pilkonis, P., . . . Kupfer, D. J. (2004). Personality pathology and outcome in recurrently depressed women over 2 years of maintenance interpersonal psychotherapy. *Psychological Medicine, 34,* 659–669.

David-Ferdon, C., & Kaslow, N. (2008). Evidence-based psychological treatments for child and adolescent depression. *Journal of Clinical Child and Adolescent Psychology, 37*(1), 62–104.

de Mello, M. F., Myczcowisk, L. M., & Menezes, P. R. (2001). A randomized controlled trial comparing moclobemide and moclobemide plus interpersonal therapy in the treatment of dysthymic disorder. *The Journal of Psychotherapy Practice and Research, 10*(2), 117–123.

Devlin, M. J., Goldfein, J. A., Petkova, E., Jiang, H., Raizman, P. S., Wolk, S., . . . Walsh, B. T. (2005). Cognitive behavioral therapy and fluoxetine as adjuncts to group behavioral therapy for binge eating disorder. *Obesity Research, 13*(6), 1077–1088.

Dietz, L., Mufson, L., Irvine, H., & Brent, D. (2008). Family-based interpersonal psychotherapy for depressed preadolescents: An open-treatment trial. *Early Intervention in Psychiatry, 2,* 180–187.

DiMascio, A., Weissman, M. M., Prusoff, B. A., Neu, C., Zwilling, M., & Klerman, G. L. (1979). Differential symptom reduction by drugs and psychotherapy in acute depression. *Archives of General Psychiatry, 36,* 1450–1456

Elkin, I., Shea, T., Watkins, J. T., Imber, S. D., Sotsky, S. M., Collins, J. F., . . . Parloff, M. B. (1989). National Institute of Mental Health Treatment of Depression Collaborative Research Program. *Archives of General Psychiatry, 46* (November), 971–982.

Fairburn, C. G., Jones, R., Peveler, R. C., Carr, S. J., Solomon, R. A., O'Connor, M. E., . . . Hope R. A. (1991). Three psychological treatments for bulimia nervosa. *Archives of General Psychiatry, 48*, 463–469.

Fairburn, C. G., Jones, R., Peveler, R. C., Hope, R. A., & O'Connor, M. (1993). Psychotherapy and bulimia nervosa. Longer-term effects of interpersonal psychotherapy, behavior therapy, and cognitive behavior therapy. *Archives of General Psychiatry, 50*(6), 419–428.

Feske, U., Frank, E., Kupfer, D. J., Shear, M. K., & Weaver, E. (1998). Anxiety as a predictor of response to interpersonal psychotherapy for recurrent major depression: An exploratory investigation. *Depression and Anxiety, 8*, 135–141.

Fickenscher, A., Lipidus, J., Silk-Walker, P., & Becker, T. (2001). Women behind bars: Health needs of inmates in a county jail. *Public Health Reports, 116*, 191–196.

Frank, E. (1991). Interpersonal psychotherapy as a maintenance treatment for patients with recurrent depression. *Psychotherapy and Psychosomatics, 28*(2), 259–266.

Frank, E. (2005). *Treating bipolar disorder: A clinician's guide to interpersonal and social rhythm therapy.* New York, NY: Guilford Press.

Frank, E., Frank, N., Cornes, C. L., Imber, S. D., Miller, M., Morris, S., & Reynolds, C. F. (1993). Interpersonal psychotherapy in the treatment of late-life depression. In G. L. Klerman & M. M. Weissman (Eds.), *New applications of interpersonal psychotherapy.* Washington, DC: American Psychiatric Press.

Frank, E., Grochocinski, V. J., Spanier, C. A., Buysse, D. J., Cherry, C. R., Houck, P. R., . . . Kupfer, D. J. (2000). Interpersonal psychotherapy and antidepressant medication: Evaluation of sequential treatment strategy in women with recurrent major depression. *Journal of Clinical Psychiatry, 61*, 51–57.

Frank, E., Kupfer, D. J., Buysse, D., Swartz, H. A., Pilkonis, P. A., Houck, P. R., . . . Stapf, D. M. (2007). Randomized trial of weekly, twice-monthly, and monthly interpersonal psychotherapy as maintenance treatment for women with recurrent depression. *The American Journal of Psychiatry, 164*(5), 761–767.

Frank, E., Kupfer, D. J., Perel, J. M., Cornes, C., Jarrett, D. B., Mallinger, A. G., . . . Grochocinski, V. J. (1990). Three-year outcomes for maintenance therapies in recurrent depression. *Archives of General Psychiatry, 47*, 1093–1099.

Frank, E., Kupfer, D. J., Thase, M. E., Mallinger, A. G., Swartz, H. A., Fagiolini, A. M., . . . Monk, T. (2005). Two-year outcomes for interpersonal and social rhythm therapy in individuals with bipolar I disorder. *Archives of General Psychiatry, 62*(9), 996–1004.

Frank, E., Kupfer, D. J., Wagner, E. F., McEachran, A. B., & Cornes, C. (1991). Efficacy of interpersonal psychotherapy as a maintenance treatment of recurrent depression. Contributing factors. *Archives of General Psychiatry, 48*(12), 1053–1059.

Frank, E., & Novick, D. (2001). Progress in the psychotherapy of mood disorders: Studies from the Western Psychiatric Institute and Clinic. *Epidemiology and Social Psychiatry, 10*, 245–252.

Frank, E., Shear, M. K., Rucci, P., Cyranowski, J. M., Endicott, J., Fagiolini, A., . . . Cassano, M. D. (2000). Influence of panic-agoraphobic spectrum symptoms on treatment response in patients with recurrent major depression. *The American Journal of Psychiatry, 157*(7), 1101–1107.

Frank, E., & Spanier, C. A. (1995). Interpersonal psychotherapy for depression: Overview, clinical efficacy, and future directions. *Clinical Psychology: Science and Practice, 2*, 349–369.

Frank, E., Thase, M. E., Spanier, C., Cyranowski, J. M., & Siegel, L. (2000). Psychotherapy of affective disorders. In F. Henn, H. Sartorius, H. Helmchen, & H. Lauter (Eds.), *Contemporary psychiatry: Specific psychiatric disorders* (Vol. 3). Berlin/ Heidelberg, Germany: Springer-Verlag.

Grigoriadis, S., & Ravitz, P. (2007). An approach to interpersonal psychotherapy for postpartum depression. *Canadian Family Physician, 53*, 1469–1475.

Grote, N. K., Bledsoe, S. E., Swartz, H. A., & Frank, E. (2004). Culturally relevant psychotherapy for perinatal depression in low-income OB-GYN patients. *Clinical Social Work Journal, 32*(3), 327–347.

Grote, N. K., Swartz, H. A., Geibel, S. L., Zuckoff, A., Houck, P. R., & Frank, E. (2009). A randomized controlled trial of culturally relevant, brief interpersonal psychotherapy for perinatal depression. *Psychiatric Services, 60*(3), 313–321.

Henderson, S., Byrne, G., Duncan-Jones, P., Scott, R., & Adcock, S. (1980). Social relationships, adversity and neurosis: A study of associations in a general population sample. *British Journal of Psychiatry, 136*, 574–583.

Hlastala, S. A., & Frank, E. (2006). Adapting interpersonal and social rhythm therapy to the developmental needs of adolescents with bipolar disorder. *Development and Psychopathology, 18*, 1267–1288.

Hlastala, S. A., Kottler, J. S., McClellan, J. M., & McCauley, E. A. (2010). Interpersonal and social rhythm therapy for adolescents with bipolar disorder: Treatment development and results from an open trial. *Depression and Anxiety, 27*(5), 457–464.

Hollon, S. D., Jarrett, D. B., Nierenberg, A. A., Thase, M. E., Madhukar, T., & Rush, J. (2005). Psychotherapy and medication in the treatment of adult and geriatric depression: Which monotherapy or combined treatment? *The Journal of Clinical Psychiatry, 66*(4), 455–468.

Holtfreter, K., & Morash, M. (2003). The needs of women offenders: Implications for correctional programming. *Women and Criminal Justice, 14,* 137–160.

Honkalampi, K., Saarinen, P., Hintikka, J., Virtanen, V., & Viinamaki, H. (1999). Factors associated with alexithymia in patients suffering from depression. *Psychotherapy and Psychosomatics, 68,* 270–275.

Horowitz, L., Rosenberg, T. E., Baer, B., Ureño, G., & Villaseñor, V. (1988). Inventory of interpersonal problems: Psychometric properties and clinical application. *Journal of Consulting and Clinical Psychology, 56*(6), 885–892.

Jones, R., Peveler, R. C., Hope, R. A., & Fairburn, C. G. (1993). Changes during treatment for bulimia nervosa: A comparison of three psychological treatments. *Behaviour Research and Therapy, 31*(5), 479–485.

Klerman, G. L., Dimascio, A., Weissman, M. M., Prusoff, B., & Paykel, E. S. (1974). Treatment of depression by drugs and psychotherapy. *The American Journal of Psychiatry, 131*(2), 186–191.

Klerman, G. L., & Weissman, M. M. (Eds.). (1993). *New applications of interpersonal psychotherapy.* Washington, DC: American Psychiatric Press.

Klerman, G. L., Weissman, M. M., Rounsaville, B. J., & Chevron, E. S. (1984). *Interpersonal psychotherapy of depression.* New York, NY: Basic Books.

Klerman, G. L., & Weissmann, M. M. (1987). Interpersonal psychotherapy (IPT) and drugs in the treatment of depression. *Pharmacopsychiatry, 20,* 3–7.

Klier, C. M., Muzik, M., Rosenblum, K. L., & Lenz, G. (2001). Interpersonal psychotherapy adapted for the group setting in the treatment of postpartum depression. *Journal of Psychotherapy Practice and Research, 10*(2), 124–131.

Koszycki, D., Lafontaine, S., Frasure-Smith, N., Swenson, R., & Lesperance, F. (2004). An open-label trial of interpersonal psychotherapy in depressed patients with coronary disease. *Psychosomatics, 45*(4), 319–324.

Lanza di Scalea, T., Cyranowski, J. M., Gilbert, A., Siracusano, A., & Frank, E. (2006). *The role of alexithymia in patients with depression and panic disorder: A psychotherapeutic perspective.* Unpublished manuscript.

Lesperance, F., Frasure-Smith, N., Koszycki, D., Laliberte, M. A., van Zyl, L. T., Baker, B., . . . Guertin, M. C. (2007). Effects of citalopram and interpersonal psychotherapy on depression in patients with coronary artery disease: The Canadian Cardiac Randomized Evaluation of Antidepressant and Psychotherapy Efficacy (CREATE) trial. *Journal of the American Medical Association, 297*(4), 367–379.

Lipsitz, J. D., Gur, M., Miller, N. L., Forand, N., Vermes, D., & Fyer, A. J. (2006). An open pilot study of interpersonal psychotherapy for panic disorder (IPT-PD). *The Journal of Nervous and Mental Disease, 194*(6), 440–445.

Lipsitz, J. D., Gur, M., Vermes, D., Petkova, E., Cheng, J., Miller, N., . . . Fyer, A. J. (2008). A randomized trial of interpersonal therapy versus supportive therapy for social anxiety disorder. *Depression and Anxiety, 25,* 542–553.

Lipsitz, J. D., Markowitz, J. C., & Cherry, S. (1997). *Manual for interpersonal psychotherapy of social phobia.* Unpublished manuscript, Columbia University College of Physicians and Surgeons, New York, NY.

Lumley, M. A. (2000). Alexithymia and negative emotional conditions. *Journal of Psychosomatic Research, 49,* 51–54.

MacKenzie, K. R., & Grabovac, A. D. (2001). Interpersonal psychotherapy group (IPT-G) for depression. *Journal of Psychotherapy Practice and Research, 10*(1), 46–51.

Markowitz, J. C. (1996). Psychotherapy for dysthymic disorder. *Psychiatric Clinics of North America, 19,* 133–149.

Markowitz, J. C. (1998). *Interpersonal psychotherapy for dysthymic disorder.* Washington, DC: American Psychiatric Press.

Markowitz, J. C., Bleiberg, K. L., Christos, P., & Levitan, E. (2006). Solving interpersonal problems correlates with symptom improvement in interpersonal psychotherapy. *The Journal of Nervous and Mental Disease, 194*(1), 15–20.

Markowitz, J. C., Klerman, G. L., Perry, S. W., Clougherty, K. F., & Josephs, L. S. (1993). Interpersonal psychotherapy for depressed HIV-seropositive patients. In G. L. Klerman & M. M. Weissman (Eds.), *New applications of interpersonal psychotherapy.* Washington, DC: American Psychiatric Press.

Markowitz, J. C., Kocsis, J. H., Bleiberg, K. L., Christos, P. J., & Sacks, M. (2005). A comparative trial of psychotherapy and pharmacotherapy for "pure" dysthymic patients. *Journal of Affective Disorders, 89,* 167–175.

Markowitz, J. C., Kocsis, J. H., Christos, P., Bleiberg, K., & Carlin, A. (2008). Pilot study of interpersonal psychotherapy versus supportive psychotherapy for dysthymic patients with secondary alcohol abuse or dependence. *The Journal of Nervous and Mental Disease, 196*(6), 468–474.

Markowitz, J. C., Kocsis, J. H., Fishman, B., Spielman, L. A., Jacobsberg, L. B., Frances, A. J., . . . Perry, S. W. (1998). Treatment of depressive symptoms in human immunodeficiency virus-positive patients. *Archives of General Psychiatry, 55*(5), 452–457.

Markowitz, J. C., Skodol, A. E., & Bleiberg, K. (2006). Interpersonal psychotherapy for borderline personality disorder: Possible mechanisms of change. *Journal of Clinical Psychology, 62*(4), 431–444.

Markowitz, J. C., Spielman, L. A., Sullivan, M., & Fishman, B. (2000). An exploratory study of ethnicity and psychotherapy outcome among HIV-positive patients with depressive symptoms. *The Journal of Psychotherapy Practice and Research, 9*(4), 226–231.

Markowitz, J. C., & Swartz, H. A. (2007). Case formulation in interpersonal psychotherapy of depression. In T. D. Eels (Ed.), *Handbook of Psychotherapy Case Formulation* (2nd ed., pp. 221–250). New York, NY: Guilford Press.

Markowitz, J. C., & Weissman, M. M. (2004). Interpersonal psychotherapy: Principles and applications. *World Psychiatry, 3*(3), 136–139.

Mason, B. J., Markowitz, J. C., & Klerman, G. L. (1993). Interpersonal psychotherapy for dysthymic disorders. In G. L. Klerman & M. M. Weissman (Eds.), *New Applications of Interpersonal Psychotherapy*. Washington, DC: American Psychiatric Press.

McIntosh, V. V., Bulik, C. M., McKenzie, J. M., Luty, S. E., & Jordan, J. (2000). Interpersonal psychotherapy for anorexia nervosa. *The International Journal of Eating Disorders, 27*(2), 125–139.

Meyer, A. (1957). *Psychobiology: A science of man*. Springfield, IL: Charles C Thomas.

Miklowitz, D. (2008). Bipolar disorder. A family-focused treatment approach (2nd ed.). New York, NY: Guilford Press

Miklowitz, D. J., & Goldstein, M. J. (1997). *Bipolar disorder: A family-focused treatment approach*. New York, NY: Guilford.

Miklowitz, D. J., Otto, M. W., Frank, E., Reilly-Harrington, N. A., Kogan, J. N., Sachs, G. S., . . . Wisniewski, S. R. (2007). Intensive psychosocial intervention enhances functioning in patients with bipolar depression: Results from a 9-month randomized controlled trial. *The American Journal of Psychiatry, 164*(9), 1340–1347.

Miklowitz, D. J., Otto, M. W., Frank, E., Reilly-Harrington, N. A., Wisniewski, S. R., Kogan, J. N., . . . Sachs, G. S. (2007). Psychosocial treatments for bipolar depression: A 1-year randomized trial from the systematic treatment enhancement program. *Archives of General Psychiatry, 64*, 419–427.

Miller, L., Gur, M., Shanok, A., & Weissman, M. (2008). Interpersonal psychotherapy with pregnant adolescents: Two pilot studies. *Journal of Child Psychology and Psychiatry, 49*(7), 733–742.

Miller, M. D. (2008). Using interpersonal therapy (IPT) with older adults today and tomorrow: A review of the literature and new developments. *Current Psychiatry Reports, 10*, 16–22.

Miller, M. D., Frank, E., Cornes, C. L., Imber, S. D., Anderson, B., Ehrenpreis, L., . . . Reynolds, C. F., III. (1994). Applying interpersonal psychotherapy to bereavement related depression following loss of a spouse in late-life. *The Journal of Psychotherapy Practice and Research, 3*, 149–162.

Monk, T., Frank, E., Potts, J. M., & Kupfer, D. J. (2002). A simple way to measure daily lifestyle regularity. *Journal of Sleep Research, 11*, 183–190.

Mufson, L., Dorta, K. P., Moreau, D., & Weissman, M. M. (2004). *Interpersonal psychotherapy for depressed adolescents* (2nd ed.). New York, NY: Guilford Press.

Mufson, L., Dorta, K. P., Wickramaratne, P., Nomura, Y., Olfson, M., & Weissman, M. M. (2004). A randomized effectiveness trial of interpersonal psychotherapy for depressed adolescents. *Archives of General Psychiatry, 61*, 577–584.

Mufson, L., & Fairbanks, J. (1996). Interpersonal psychotherapy for depressed adolescents: A one year naturalistic follow-up study. *Journal of the American Academy of Child and Adolescent Psychiatry 35*(9), 1145–1155.

Mufson, L., Gallagher, T., Dorta, K. P., & Young, J. F. (2004). A group adaptation of interpersonal psychotherapy for depressed adolescents. *American Journal of Psychotherapy, 58*(2), 220–237.

Mufson, L., Moreau, D., Weissman, M. M., & Klerman, G. L. (1993). *Interpersonal psychotherapy for depressed adolescents*. New York, NY: Guilford Press.

Mufson, L., Moreau, D., Weissman, M. M., Wickramaratne, P., Martin, J., & Samoilov, A. (1994). Modification of interpersonal psychotherapy with depressed adolescents (IPT-A): Phase I and II studies. *Journal of the American Academy of Child and Adolescent Psychiatry, 33*(5), 695–705.

Mufson, L., Weissman, M. M., Moreau, D., & Garfinkel, R. (1999). Efficacy of interpersonal psychotherapy for depressed adolescents. *Archives of General Psychiatry, 56*(6), 573–579.

O'Hara, M., Stuart, S., Gorman, L. L., & Wenzel, A. (2000). Efficacy of interpersonal psychotherapy for postpartum depression. *Archives of General Psychiatry, 57*, 1039–1045.

Ogrodniczuk, J. S., Piper, W. E., & Joyce, A. S. (2004). Alexithymia as a predictor of residual symptoms in depressed patients who respond to short-term psychotherapy. *American Journal of Psychotherapy, 58*(2), 150–161.

Parsons, T. (1951). Illness and the role of the physician: A sociological perspective. *The American Journal of Orthopsychiatry, 21*(3), 452–460.

Pearlstein, T. B., Zlotnick, C., Battle, C. L., Stuart, S., O'Hara, M. W., Price, A. B., . . . Howard, M. (2006). Patient choice of treatment for postpartum depression: A pilot study. *Archives of Women's Mental Health, 9*, 303–308.

Phillips, K. A. (1996). *The broken mirror: Understanding and treating body dysmorphic disorder.* New York, NY: Oxford University Press.

Phillips, K. A., & Diaz, S. F. (1997). Gender differences in body dysmorphic disorder. *Journal of Nervous and Mental Disease, 185*(9), 570–577.

Phillips, K. A., & McElroy, S. L. (2000). Personality disorders and traits in patients with body dysmorphic disorder. *Comprehensive Psychiatry, 41*(4), 229–236.

Phillips, K. A., McElroy, S. L., Hudson, J. I., & Pope, H. G., Jr. (1995). Body dysmorphic disorder: an obsessive compulsive spectrum disorder, a form of affective spectrum disorder, or both? *Journal of Clinical Psychiatry, 56*(4), 41–52.

Phillips, K. A., McElroy, S. L., Keck, P. E., Jr. Pope, H. G., Jr. & Hudson, J. I. (1993). Body dysmorphic disorder: 30 cases of imagined ugliness. *The American Journal of Psychiatry, 150*(2), 302–308.

Phillips, K. A., Nierenberg, A. A., Brendel, G., & Fava, M. (1996). Prevalence and clinical features of body dysmorphic disorder in atypical major depression. *Journal of Nervous and Mental Disease, 184*, 125–129.

Phillips, K. A., Pinto, A., & Jain, S. (2004). Self-esteem in body dysmorphic disorder. *Body Image: An International Journal of Research, 1*, 385–390.

Pilkonis, P. A., & Frank, E. (1988). Personality pathology in recurrent depression: Nature, prevalence, and relationship to treatment response. *American Journal of Psychiatry, 145*(4).

Reay, R., Fisher, Y., Robertson, M., Adams, E., & Owen, C. (2006). Group interpersonal psychotherapy for postnatal depression: A pilot study. *Archives of Women's Mental Health, 9*, 31–39.

Reynolds, C. F., Frank, E., Perel, J. M., Imber, S. D., Cornes, C., Miller, M. D., . . . Kupfer, D. J. (1999). Nortriptyline and interpersonal psychotherapy as maintenance therapies for recurrent major depression. *The Journal of American Medical Association, 281*(1), 139–145.

Robertson, M., Rushton, P., Batrim, D., Moore, E., & Morris, P. (2007). Open trial of interpersonal psychotherapy for chronic post traumatic stress disorder. *Australian Psychiatry, 15*(5), 375–379.

Robertson, M., Rushton, P. J., Bartrum, D., & Ray, R. (2004). Group-based interpersonal psychotherapy for posttraumatic stress disorder: Theoretical and clinical aspects. *International Journal of Group Psychotherapy, 54*(2), 145–175.

Rockland, L. H. (1992). Psychodynamically oriented supportive therapy. In *Supportive therapy for borderline patients: A psychodynamic approach*. New York, NY: Guilford Press.

Rosselló, J., & Bernal, G. (1999). The efficacy of cognitive–behavioral and interpersonal treatments for depression in Puerto Rican adolescents. *Journal of Consulting and Clinical Psychology, 67*(5), 734–745.

Rothblum, E., Sholomskas, A., Berry, C., & Prusoff, B. A. (1982). Issues in clinical trials with the depressed elderly. *Journal of American Geriatric Society, 30*(11), 694–699.

Rounsaville, B., Gawin, F., & Kleber, H. (1985). Interpersonal psychotherapy adapted for ambulatory cocaine abusers. *American Journal of Drug and Alcohol Abuse, 11*(3–4), 171–191.

Rounsaville, B. J., Glazer, W., Wilber, C. H., Weissman, M. M., & Kleber, H. D. (1983). Short-term interpersonal psychotherapy in methadone-maintained opiate addicts. *Archives of General Psychiatry, 40*(6), 629–636.

Schneider, L. S., Sloane, R. B., Staples, F. R., & Bender, M. (1986). Pretreatment orthostatic hypotension as a predictor of response to nortiptyline in geriatric depression. *Journal of Clinical Psychopharmacology, 6*(3), 172–176.

Schramm, E., van Calker, D., Dykierek, P., Lieb, K., Kech, S., Zobel, I., . . . Berger, M. (2007). An intensive treatment program of interpersonal psychotherapy plus pharmacotherapy for depressed in patients: Acute and long term results. *The American Journal of Psychiatry, 164*(5), 768–777.

Schulberg, H. C., Scott, C. P., Madonia, M. J., & Imber, S. D. (1993). Applications of interpersonal psychotherapy to depression in primary care practice. In G. L. Klerman & M. M. Weissman (Eds.), *New applications of interpersonal psychotherapy*. Washington, DC: American Psychiatric Press.

Shea, M. T., Pilkonis, P. A., Beckham, E., Collins, J. F., Elkin, I., Sotsky, S. M., . . . Docherty, J. P. (1990). Personality disorders and treatment outcome in the NIMH Treatment of Depression Collaborative Research Program. *The American Journal of Psychiatry, 147*(6), 711–718.

Shear, M. K., Rucci, P., Grochocinski, V., Vanderbilt, J., & Houck, P. R. (2001). Reliability and validity of the panic disorder severity scale: Replication and extension. *Journal of Psychiatric Research, 35*, 293–296.

Sholomskas, A. J., Chevron, E. S., Prusoff, B. A., & Berry, C. (1983). Short-term inter-personal therapy (IPT) with the depressed elderly: Case reports and discussion. *American Journal of Psychotherapy, 37*(4), 552–566.

Sloane, R. B., Staples, F. R., & Schneider, L. S. (1985). Interpersonal therapy versus nortriptyline for depression in the elderly. In G. Burrows, T. R. Norman & L. Dennerstein (Eds.), *Clinical and pharmacological studies in psychiatric disorders* (pp. 344–346). London, England: John Libbey.

Sotsky, S. M., Glass, D. R., Shea, M. T., Pilkonis, P. A., Collins, J. F., Elkin, I., . . . Moyer, J. (1991). Patient predictors of response to psychotherapy and phar-macotherapy: Findings in the NIMH treatment of depression collaborative research program. *American Journal of Psychiatry, 148*(8), 997–1008.

Spinelli, M. G., & Endicott, J. (2003). Controlled clinical trial of interpersonal psy-chotherapy versus parenting education program for depressed pregnant women. *The American Journal of Psychiatry, 160*, 555–562.

Steiner, M., Browne, G. J. R., Gafni, A., Byrne, C., Bell, B., & Dunn, E. (1998). *Sertraline and IPT in dysthymia: One year follow-up.* Paper presented at the 38th Annual Meeting of the NIMH New Clinical Drug Evaluation Unit (NCDEU), Boca Raton, FL.

Stuart, S., & O'Hara, M. W. (1995). Interpersonal psychotherapy for postpartum depression. *The Journal of Psychotherapy Practice and Research, 4*, 18–29.

Stuart, S., & Robertson, M. (2003). *Interpersonal psychotherapy: A clinician's guide.* New York, NY: Oxford University Press.

Substance Abuse and Mental Health Services Administration. (1999). *Substance abuse treatment for women offenders: Guide to promising practices.* Rockville, MD: Author.

Sullivan, H. S. (1953). *The interpersonal theory of psychiatry.* New York, NY: Norton.

Swartz, H. A., Frank, E., Frankel, D. R., Novick, D., & Houck, P. R. (2009). Psycho-therapy as monotherapy for the treatment of bipolar II depression: A proof of concept study. *Bipolar Disorders, 11*, 89–94.

Swartz, H., Frank, E., Zuckoff, A., Cyranowski, J. M., Houck, P. R., Cheng, Y., . . . Shear, M. K. (2008). Brief interpersonal psychotherapy for depressed mothers whose children are receiving psychiatric treatment. *The American Journal of Psychiatry, 165*, 1155–1162.

Swartz, H. A., Markowitz, J. C., & Frank, E. (2002). Interpersonal psychotherapy for unipolar and bipolar disorders. In S. Hoffmann & M. Tompson (Eds.), *Treating chronic and severe mental disorders: A handbook of empirically supported interventions.* New York, NY: Guilford Press.

Swartz, H. A., Zuckoff, A., Frank, E., Spielvogle, H. N., Shear, M. K., Fleming, D., . . . Scott, J. (2006). An open-label trial of enhanced brief interpersonal psychotherapy in depressed mothers whose children are receiving psychiatric treatment. *Depression and Anxiety, 23,* 398–404.

Talbot, N. L., Conwell, Y., O'Hara, M. W., Stuart, S., Ward, E. A., Gamble, S. A., . . . Tu, X. (2005). Interpersonal psychotherapy for depressed women with sexual abuse histories: A pilot study in a community mental health center. *Journal of Nervous and Mental Disease, 193,* 847–850.

Tanofsky-Kraff, M. (2008). Binge eating among children and adolescents. In E. Jelalian & R. Steele (Eds.), *Handbook of child and adolescent obesity* (pp. 41–57). New York, NY: Springer.

Tanofsky-Kraff, M., Wilfley, D. E., Young, J. F., Mufson, L., Yanovski, S. Z., Glasofer, D. R., . . . Salaita, C. G. (2007). Preventing excessive weight gain in adolescents: Interpersonal psychotherapy for binge eating. *Obesity (Silver Spring), 15*(6), 1345–1355.

Tanofsky-Kraff, M., Yanovski, S. Z., Schvey, N. A., Olsen, C., Gustafson, J., & Yanovski, J. A. (2009). A prospective study of loss of control eating for body weight gain in children at high-risk for adult obesity. *International Journal of Eating Disorders, 42*(1), 26–30.

Thase, M. E. (1996). The role of axis II comorbidity in the management of patients with treatment-resistant depression. *The Psychiatric Clinics of North America, 19*(2), 287–309.

U. S. Department of Justice. (1999). *Women offenders.* Washington, DC: Bureau of Justice Statistics Clearinghouse.

Vanhuele, S., Desmet, M., Meganck, R., & Bogaerts, S. (2007). Alexithymia and interpersonal problems. *Journal of Clinical Psychology, 63*(1), 109–117.

Verdeli, H., Clougherty, K., Bolton, P., Speelman, L., Ndogoni, L., Bass, J., . . . Weissman, M. M. (2003). Adapting group interpersonal psychotherapy for a developing country: Experience in rural Uganda. *World Psychiatry, 2*(2), 114–120.

Weissman, M. M. (2006). A brief history of interpersonal psychotherapy. *Psychiatric Annals, 36,* 553–557

Weissman, M. M., Klerman, G. L., Paykel, E. S., Prusoff, B., & Hanson, B. (1974). Treatment effects on the social adjustment of depressed patients. *Archives of General Psychiatry, 30*(6), 771–778.

Weissman, M. M., Klerman, G. L., Prusoff, B. A., Sholomskas, D., & Padian, N. (1981). Depressed outpatients: Results one year after treatment with drugs and/or interpersonal psychotherapy. *Archives of General Psychiatry, 38*, 51–55.

Weissman, M. M., & Markowitz, J. C. (1994). Interpersonal psychotherapy: Current status. *Archives of General Psychiatry, 51*, 599–606.

Weissman, M. M., Markowitz, J. C., & Klerman, G. L. (2000). *Comprehensive guide to interpersonal psychotherapy*. New York, NY: Basic Books.

Weissman, M. M., Markowitz, J. C., & Klerman, G. L. (2007). *Clinician's quick guide to interpersonal psychotherapy*. New York, NY: Oxford University Press.

Weissman, M. M., Verdeli, H., Gameroff, M. J., Bledsoe, S. E., Betts, K., Mufson, L., ... Wickramaratne, P. (2006). National survey of psychotherapy training in psychiatry, psychology, and social work. *Archives of General Psychiatry, 63*, 925–934.

Wilfley, D. E., Agras, W. S., Telch, C. F., Rossiter, E. M., Schneider, J. A., Cole, A. G., ... Raeburn, S. D. (1993). Group cognitive–behavioral therapy and group interpersonal psychotherapy for the nonpurging bulimic individual: A controlled comparison. *Journal of Consulting and Clinical Psychology, 61*(2), 296–305.

Wilfley, D. E., MacKenzie, K. R., Welch, R. R., Ayres, V. E., & Weissman, M. M. (2000). *Interpersonal Psychotherapy for Group*. New York, NY: Basic Books.

Wilfley, D. E., Welch, R. R., Stein, R. I., Spurrell, E. B., Cohen, L. R., Saelens, B. E., ... Matt, G. E. (2002). A randomized comparison of group cognitive–behavioral therapy and group interpersonal psychotherapy for the treatment of overweight individuals with binge-eating disorder. *Archives of General Psychiatry, 59*(8), 713–721.

Young, J. F., & Mufson, L. (2003). *Manual for interpersonal psychotherapy-adolescent skills training (IPT-AST)*. New York, NY: Columbia University.

Young, J. F., Mufson, L., & Davies, M. (2006). Efficacy of interpersonal psychotherapy-adolescent skills training: An indicated preventive intervention for depression. *Journal of Child Psychology and Psychiatry, 47*(12), 1254–1262.

Zuckerman, D. M., Prusoff, B. A., Weissman, M. M., & Padian, N. S. (1980). Personality as a predictor of psychotherapy and pharmacotherapy outcome for depression outpatients. *Journal of Consulting and Clinical Psychology, 48*(6), 730–735.

Index

About the Authors

Ellen Frank, PhD, is a distinguished professor of psychiatry and a professor of psychology at the University of Pittsburgh School of Medicine and director of the Depression and Manic-Depression Prevention Program at the Western Psychiatric Institute and Clinic of the University of Pittsburgh Medical Center. She completed her undergraduate work in drama at Vassar College in Poughkeepsie, New York, completed a master's degree in English at Carnegie-Mellon University in Pittsburgh, Pennsylvania, and obtained her PhD in psychology at the University of Pittsburgh. She received her training in interpersonal psychotherapy (IPT) from Drs. Gerald Klerman, Myrna Weissman, and Bruce Rounsaville in the early 1980s. Since that time Dr. Frank and her colleagues have developed a series of adaptations of IPT, including those for preventative maintenance treatment of unipolar depression and for the acute and maintenance treatment of bipolar disorder, each of which they have subsequently validated in empirical studies.

Jessica C. Levenson, MS, is a PhD candidate in clinical psychology at the University of Pittsburgh. She received a BA from Brandeis University in Waltham, Massachusetts, and an MS from the University of Pittsburgh. Ms. Levenson's work focuses on the mechanistic understanding and treatment of mood disorders. Her recent work has focused on identifying the patient and treatment characteristics that may differentiate those patients who benefit most from interpersonal psychotherapy.

About the Series Editors

Jon Carlson, PsyD, EdD, ABPP, is distinguished professor of psychology and counseling at Governors State University in University Park, Illinois, and a psychologist at the Wellness Clinic in Lake Geneva, Wisconsin. Dr. Carlson has served as the editor of several periodicals, including the *Journal of Individual Psychology* and *The Family Journal*. He holds diplomas in both family psychology and Adlerian psychology. He has authored 150 journal articles and 40 books, including *Time for a Better Marriage, Adlerian Therapy, The Mummy at the Dining Room Table, Bad Therapy, The Client Who Changed Me,* and *Moved by the Spirit*. He has created more than 200 professional trade videos and DVDs with leading professional therapists and educators. In 2004 the American Counseling Association named him a "Living Legend." Recently he syndicated the advice cartoon *On The Edge* with cartoonist Joe Martin.

Matt Englar-Carlson, PhD, is an associate professor of counseling at California State University, Fullerton, and an adjunct senior lecturer in the School of Health at the University of New England in Armidale, Australia. He is a fellow of Division 51 of the American Psychological Association (APA). As a scholar, teacher, and clinician, Dr. Englar-Carlson has been an innovator and is professionally passionate about training and teaching clinicians to work more effectively with their male clients. He has more than 30 publications and 50 national and international presentations, most of which are focused on men and masculinity. Dr. Englar-Carlson coedited the books *In the Room With Men: A Casebook of Therapeutic Change* and *Counseling Troubled Boys: A Guidebook for Professionals.* In 2007 he was named the Researcher of the Year by the Society for the Psychological Study of Men and Masculinity. He is also a member of the APA Working Group to Develop Guidelines for Psychological Practice With Boys and Men. As a clinician, he has worked with children, adults, and families in school, community, and university mental health settings.